THE
TIPSY
VEGAN

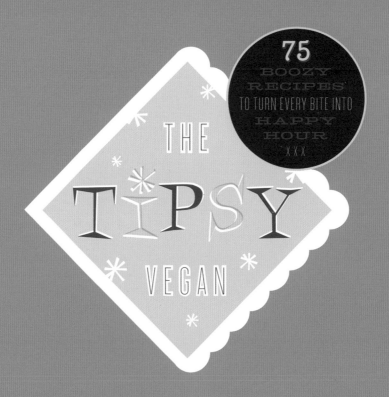

THE TIPSY VEGAN

75 BOOZY RECIPES TO TURN EVERY BITE INTO HAPPY HOUR xxx

JOHN SCHLIMM

PHOTOGRAPHS BY AMY BEADLE ROTH

Da Capo
LIFE
LONG

A Member of the Perseus Books Group

Copyright © 2011 by John E. Schlimm II
Photographs Copyright © 2011 by Amy Beadle Roth

Design and production by Megan Jones Design (www.meganjonesdesign.com)
Illustration by Tim McGrath

Library of Congress Cataloging-in-Publication Data

Schlimm, John E., 1971–
  The tipsy vegan : 75 recipes to turn every bite into happy hour / John Schlimm ; photographs by Amy Beadle Roth.—1st Da Capo Press ed.
      p. cm.
  Includes bibliographical references and index.
    ISBN 978-0-7382-1507-5 (pbk.)—ISBN 978-0-7382-1538-9 (e-book) 1. Vegan cooking. 2. Cooking (Liquors) 3. Cookbooks. I. Title.
  TX837.S315 2011
  641.5'636—dc22
                                    2011008710

First Da Capo Press edition 2011
ISBN: 978-0-7382-1507-5

Published by Da Capo Press
A Member of the Perseus Books Group
www.dacapopress.com

Da Capo Press books are available at special discounts for bulk purchases in the United States by corporations, institutions, and other organizations. For more information, please contact the Special Markets Department at the Perseus Books Group, 2300 Chestnut Street, Suite 200, Philadelphia, PA, 19103, or call (800) 810-4145, ext. 5000, or e-mail special.markets@perseusbooks.com.

TO ALL THE ANIMALS —
SO YOU KNOW THAT
YOU HAVE NOT PASSED
THIS WAY UNLOVED.

"REALITY IS AN ILLUSION THAT OCCURS DUE TO LACK OF ALCOHOL."

—W. C. FIELDS

THE GUZZLER'S GARDEN OF SIDE DISHES   57

BRUNCH BUZZ   83

DRUNKEN DESSERTS 135

A NOTE TO READERS

Every attempt has been made to confirm that the alcohol used throughout this book is either inherently vegan-friendly or produced in vegan-friendly forms by various brands. For more information on vegan-friendly brands of alcohol, please visit www.Barnivore.com.

In reference to the "sugar" used as an ingredient in the recipes throughout this book, regular white, refined table sugar is often made using animal bone char and avoided by vegans. Therefore, where you see "sugar" used herein, you can use vegan-friendly granulated sugars, such as the Florida Crystals brand (www.Florida Crystals.com), or other vegan-friendly sugar substitutes of choice.

Where a recipe calls for "vegan margarine" as a substitute for traditional butter, I suggest using the Earth Balance brand of buttery spreads (www.earthbalancenatural.com) or another nondairy, trans-fat-free, nonhydrogenated vegan margarine of choice.

INTRODUCTION

It's time to check reality at the door! At least for the next hundred or so pages. I'm taking you to a place where having seconds never felt so good, and the only thing cruel about satisfying your hunger is running out of liquor before you finish mixing Tequila Seduces Guacamole or Three Tomatoes to the Wind Flan, *or* before you can indulge in a Noontime Quickie.

You see, it's always Happy Hour here in the Tipsy Vegan world. And everything you need to party is now right at your fingertips, whether you're getting home at the crack of dawn, power lunching, hosting a backyard blow-out or high-falutin dinner, or scavenging for the perfect midnight snack (in which case you should *lunge* for the Chocolate-Soused Strawberries or a little Bi-Curious Orange Sorbet).

I know, I know: A lot of people think vegan food is supposed to taste like ground-up chickpeas and sand slathered on cardboard with a tofu chaser. I'd like to see those silly naysayers tell that to the Hotta Frittata with Chopped Jalapeños or Bad-Ass Beer Cake with Bourbon Raisins & Amaretto Frosting!

Whether you're a lifelong vegan, a newbie, an occasional visitor, or merely doing a little experimenting, together we're going to transform vegan cuisine from mysterious and often misunderstood into *eyes-rolled-back-in-your-head fab-u-lous*. That's right, gluttony is about to be upgraded from deadly sin to art form by the Tipsy Vegans of the world.

The gang's all here to pitch in and do their part: vodka, rum, sherry, brandy, Cointreau, tequila, cognac, amaretto, whiskey, wine, and beer, to name only a few of the A-listers at this tasty bash. They're not only for tossing down the hatch anymore, and these tipsy friends with benefits aim to please.

Throughout eight chapters, running the full course from Plastered Party Starters to Drunken Desserts, and including a buzz-worthy brunch, a lunch menu custom-made for lushes, sloshed suppers, and much more, you're going to be re-introduced to some of our oldest and dearest friends like you've never seen them before . . . in their latest incarnation as key ingredients.

To begin with, each chapter is kicked off with a high-octane cocktail to help you coast right on through prep time (Hoochie-Coochie Margarita or Extra! Extra! Dirty-Hot Martini, anyone?). As you can see, I'm a firm believer that cooking should be just as fun as eating. That's why each dish in *The Tipsy Vegan* is infused with one or more superstars from the bar circuit—to keep the good times rolling and give you one more reason to do it in the kitchen. *Bow chika YUM YUM!*

This is a loaded love-fest with recipes that are easy to prepare and what I like to call small-town friendly, meaning anyone, anywhere can whip them up. I wanted to make sure everyone, from my neighbors at home to my big city pals, can head out to their local grocery (and liquor!) store and find the ingredients they need. In a few instances, there are some special guest stars, like vegan chocolate and Vegenaise, that I was excited to share with you, especially if you've never had these little culinary gems before.

Oh, but how ever to describe the pure magic that happens when chickpeas meet cognac, pizza carouses with vodka, avocados tango with tequila, acorn squash paints the town with apple liqueur, and tofu gets down and dirty with sherry? Well, that's like trying to describe the adrenaline rush of a first kiss. Sure it feels good, sure the world spins a little, and *for sure* you can't wait to do it again.

Enjoying the spiked wonder of these dishes is more a sensation that carries you away from life as you know it than it is anything we mere mortals can explain with words. So leave it up to your taste buds to do all the talking! Trust me, life will never be the same after that first bite.

Take the Bottom's Up VegeBean Stew: The hoppy twang of the dark beer tempts the earthy flavors from the beans and vegetables, commanding your taste buds to attention while ultimately enriching and bringing the distinctively sudsy flavor profile of the entire dish full circle. (Cue the image of this hunky dreamboat headed straight for your kisser!)

See what I mean? It sure sounds delish, but you really have to wrap your mouth around it to fully appreciate and savor just how scrumptious this stew, and all the dishes you're about to meet for the first time, are.

Which brings me to my favorite part about this boozy collection: It is a celebration where everyone is welcome.

No matter who you are, where you are, or what preconceived notions you're strolling in with, I invite you to EAT, LAUGH, and PARTY like there's no tomorrow. After all, *The Tipsy Vegan* is a place where reality takes a flying leap and this very moment is all about living life to the absolute fullest!

THE TIPSY VEGAN'S LIQUOR CABINET

In the Tipsy Vegan world, the liquor cabinet is always fully stocked and ready to please. While the boozy movers and shakers below make appearances throughout the book, I am all for playing the field. Therefore, if you want to experiment by mixing and matching, swapping a swig of this for a swig of that, or by adding your own favorites to The Tipsy Vegan's Liquor Cabinet, by all means, be my guest!

AMARETTO (ALMOND LIQUEUR) [pages 86, 147]

APPLE LIQUEUR [pages 115, 120, 139, 153]

BEER [pages 113, 123]
Dark beer [pages 119, 123]
Light (reduced calorie) beer [pages 75, 107]
Pale ale [page 146]

BITTERS
Angostura Aromatic Bitters [page 79]

BRANDY [pages 8, 100, 125, 137, 156]
Calvados (apple brandy) [pages 115, 120, 139, 153]
Cognac [pages 18, 39, 50, 76, 91, 104, 137]
Kirsch (Kirschwasser) (fruit/cherry brandy)
[page 137]
Peach brandy [page 154]

CHAMPAGNE [pages 48, 49, 84]

CRÈME DE MENTHE [page 136]
AND WHITE CRÈME DE MENTHE [page 156]

FRANGELICO (HAZELNUT LIQUEUR) [page 26]

GIN [pages 118, 136]

MIDORI MELON LIQUEUR [page 30]

ORANGE LIQUEUR [page 152]
Cointreau [pages 42, 44, 60, 80, 84, 94, 137, 152]
Curaçao [page 8]
Grand Marnier [page 152]
Triple sec [pages 98, 140, 142, 152]

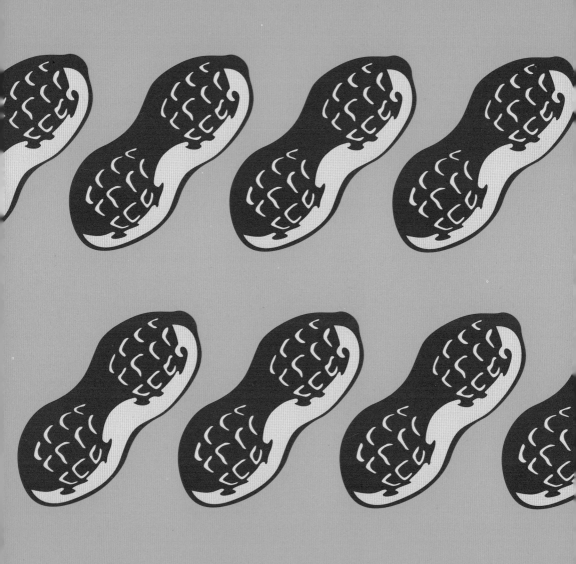

1

PLASTERED PARTY STARTERS

"The problem with the world is that everyone is a few drinks behind."

—HUMPHREY BOGART

HERE'S SOMETHING
TO GET YOU STARTED ...

Dandy Brandy Punch

Friends, *start your engines!* This potent concoction of citrus and liquor packs a wallop and will nicely kick off any celebratory gathering. So, consider yourselves forewarned: most guests will hightail it back to the punch bowl for seconds (*at least*), so plan and party accordingly.

Juice of 8 lemons

Juice of 2 oranges

¾ pound confectioners' sugar

¾ cup Curaçao

2 ounces grenadine

1¼ quarts brandy

In a large pitcher, stir all the ingredients together well. Pour the punch into a punch bowl with a large block of ice.

YIELD: 18 TO 20 CUPS

Flaming Hot Peanuts

For those who like it *hot!!!*, you've come to the right place. Have a fire extinguisher (or, in Tipsy Vegan speak, a cool cocktail) on standby and open your hatch for these blazing little dazzlers, which have been paired with a few swigs of whiskey. But, if you must, you can control the heat in this zippy snack by selecting bottled sauces with less flame. Though I plead with you to have a heart—this recipe is really intended for adventure seekers who like their kissers ignited with flavor.

2 pounds dry-roasted, salted peanuts

⅛ cup Tabasco Sauce

⅛ cup peanut oil

Juice of 1 lime

1 teaspoon sugar, or 2 teaspoons prepared
    sweet red pepper relish

¼ cup bottled crushed jalapeños, drained

3 tablespoons whiskey

8 droplets of liquid smoke (optional)

Other hot sauces of your choice to make 1 cup of liquid
    (or mild sauces for a little less kick)

Pour the peanuts into a large, resealable plastic bag. In a 1-cup glass measure, blend the remaining ingredients.

Stir the mixture thoroughly and pour over the peanuts, seal the bag, and squeeze it to mix thoroughly.

Marinate the peanuts overnight in the refrigerator, turning the bag a few times.

Preheat the oven to 250°F. Line a baking sheet or jelly roll pan with parchment paper. Spread the peanut mixture evenly over the sheet. Roast slowly for 2 to 2½ hours, stirring every half hour.

Turn the oven off, and let the peanuts rest in the closed oven overnight to dry out.

Store in airtight container(s) lined with paper towels.

YIELD: 2 POUNDS HOT PEANUTS

NOTE: Begin the recipe two days before you want to serve the peanuts.

Tequila Seduces Guacamole

What would guacamole be without a tequila chaser? ¡Ay caramba! Luckily for us, with this recipe we'll never again have to ponder that terrifying question. Share the love and mix a few tablespoons of the lively spirit directly into this classic south-of-the-border dip. Just beware the fire hazard: when adding the jalapeños, carefully taste a slice to determine the *sizzle* factor, which can vary wildly. As for the limes, usually the smoother the skin, the juicier the lime.

3 ripe Hass avocados

¼ cup fresh cilantro leaves, nicely chopped

½ medium red onion, diced

1 to 3 jalapeños (depending on your heat preferences), stemmed, seeded, and finely diced

Juice of 1 lime, about 3 tablespoons

2 to 3 tablespoons good tequila

1 teaspoon salt

½ teaspoon pepper

Lightly warmed tortilla chips, for serving

Halve the avocados and remove the pits by whacking them with a knife blade and twisting them out. Use a spoon to scrape the avocado flesh into a large mixing bowl and mash with a fork just until chunky. Add the cilantro, red onion, jalapeños, lime juice, tequila, salt, and pepper and combine with the fork. If the mixture seems too thick, add a bit more tequila. Serve at room temperature with plenty of warm tortilla chips.

YIELD: ABOUT 2 CUPS

Salsa alla Vodka

The new leader of the Salsa Kingdom has risen and is ready to serve you. This tanked twist on everyone's favorite dip can be used instead of ketchup on a veggie burger, to top off a baked potato, or as an unforgettable *backyard-tailgating-couch potato-me time-party time-anytime* dip with tortilla chips.

2 to 3 ripe red tomatoes, peeled, seeded, and roughly chopped, or 2 cups canned organic diced tomatoes, drained, if tomatoes are out of season

5 scallions, finely diced, light green and white parts only

1 medium cucumber, peeled, seeded, and diced

½ long mild chile (for example, Anaheim or poblano), or 1 green bell pepper, seeded and diced

2 tablespoons chopped cilantro leaves

2 tablespoons chopped chives

½ teaspoon sugar

Hot pepper sauce to taste

Salt and freshly ground black pepper

½ cup chilled vodka

Droplets of extra-virgin olive oil

In a large bowl, fold the tomatoes, scallions, cucumber, chile, cilantro, chives, and sugar together. Season with the hot pepper sauce, salt, and pepper, then stir in the vodka. Finish with droplets of the olive oil. Cover with plastic wrap and refrigerate until ready to serve.

YIELD: ABOUT 3 CUPS OF SALSA

sh-sh-sh-sh-sh-SHERRY BOMB! Patatas Bravas

¡Olé! A sassy splash of sherry enlivens this classic Spanish tapas, which translates to "Fierce Potatoes" and works as an appetizer or side dish. In either case, it will have you and your guests dancing in the streets until dawn.

12 small potatoes, unpeeled

2 tablespoons extra-virgin olive oil

1 tablespoon white wine vinegar

2 tablespoons dry sherry

1 pinch smoked paprika

1 clove garlic, pressed

1 teaspoon chile powder

Salt

Bring a large pan of salted water to a boil. Add the potatoes and cook for about 20 minutes, until tender but not falling apart. Drain and let cool, then peel and slice or dice. Transfer to a plate or tray. In a medium bowl, mix together the remaining ingredients. Pour the mixture over the potatoes and serve hot.

YIELD: 2 TO 4 SERVINGS

Hubba-Hubba Baba Ganoush

The famed Middle Eastern Baba Ganoush will bring an international flair to your next get-together, be it a swanky cocktail party or a backyard hoedown. And when your guests learn that your unique version of this eggplant and hummus dip is spiked with Scotch, you'll have them eating out of your hand in no time.

2 medium eggplants (about 1 to 1¼ pounds each)

3 cloves garlic, smashed

¼ cup hummus or vegan mayonnaise, such as Vegenaise

1 teaspoon salt

1 tablespoon lemon juice

2 tablespoons Scotch, or more to taste

1 teaspoon minced parsley

Pita bread wedges for serving

Heat the broiler. Place the whole eggplants on a foil-lined baking sheet. Broil the eggplants for 15 to 20 minutes, turning them every 5 minutes to char all sides, just until the eggplant is soft. Let the eggplants cool completely. Drain any juices, remove the blackened skin, and transfer the eggplant flesh to a food processor.

Add the garlic, hummus, salt, lemon juice, and Scotch. Process the mixture to the desired consistency, pulsing about 20 times for a chunkier mix or processing for 15 seconds to get smoother results. Season the Baba Ganoush with additional Scotch, lemon juice, and salt to taste. Transfer to a bowl, garnish with the minced parsley, and serve with warmed wedges of pita bread.

YIELD: ABOUT 2 CUPS

Carousing Cucumber Rounds with Rummy Hummus

These little ditties will have you and your guests spinning *round, round, round* while the good times roll. The crunchy cucumbers cool down the assertive and spicy, lightly rummy hummus, bringing balance and satisfaction to your tummy.

1 (14-ounce) can of chickpeas, rinsed and drained thoroughly

2 canned chipotle peppers, stemmed if necessary, with a teaspoon of the adobo sauce they were canned with (add more peppers, if desired)

1 large garlic clove, coarsely chopped

3 tablespoons fresh lemon juice

3 tablespoons tahini (mixed well before measuring)

2 tablespoons extra-virgin olive oil

2 tablespoons white rum (or more to taste)

1 teaspoon ground cumin

¼ teaspoon kosher salt, plus more for sprinkling

1 large English (seedless) cucumber (usually plastic-wrapped at the supermarket)

1 tablespoon sesame seeds, toasted in a dry skillet just until golden brown

In a medium bowl, place the chickpeas, chipotles, garlic, lemon juice, tahini, olive oil, white rum, cumin, and ¼ teaspoon salt. Puree with an immersion blender, scraping down the sides of the bowl as necessary, about 2 minutes, until the mixture is smooth and fluffy. Or use a standing blender (see note below).

Use a vegetable peeler to peel the cucumber skin lengthwise at ¼-inch intervals to create a striped pattern around the circumference of the cucumber and slice it crosswise into ¼-inch rounds. If the cucumber skin is tough, peel the entire cucumber. Arrange the cucumber discs on a platter.

To assemble, just before serving, lightly salt the cucumber rounds. Top each round with a generous teaspoon of hummus. Sprinkle with sesame seeds.

YIELD: ABOUT 35 HORS D'OEUVRES

NOTE: Don't be tempted to use a food processor to make this spread because you won't get that perfectly smooth texture.

Raging Chickpea Spread

Chickpea, meet your new best friend: Cognac! This dynamic duo and its accompanying cast of tasty ingredients create a spread so adaptable, so easy, so mouthwatering, you can simply serve it on flatbread and knock your guests' socks off every time.

2 (15-ounce) cans chickpeas, drained

1 (6-ounce) jar roasted red peppers, drained well and coarsely chopped

½ lemon, juiced

2 cloves garlic, pressed

2 tablespoons chopped fresh rosemary leaves

Salt and freshly ground black pepper

2 tablespoons extra-virgin olive oil

2 tablespoons cognac

1 package flatbread, sliced into bite-size pieces, or crackers of choice

1 pint grape tomatoes, rinsed and halved

1 zucchini, sliced into ¼-inch disks

In a food processor, combine the chickpeas, red peppers, lemon juice, garlic, rosemary, and pepper. Turn the processor on and stream in the olive oil, then the cognac. Transfer the smooth spread to a serving bowl on a plate and surround the bowl with the flatbread slices, halved grape tomatoes, and zucchini disks.

YIELD: ABOUT 3 CUPS OF SPREAD

Double, Double White Truffle + Trouble–Stuffed Mushrooms

The humble mushroom gets a makeover of epic proportions, with white truffle oil and Madeira, all to remind your guests that you are, indeed, *the* host or hostess with the most! The filling for these scrumptious hors d'oeuvres can be made up to a day ahead and refrigerated, giving you plenty of time to go out and discover just how fun getting in trouble can be sometimes.

1 to 2 tablespoons neutral oil, such as canola oil

20 medium white mushrooms

Salt and white pepper

2 tablespoons extra-virgin olive oil

1 medium onion, finely chopped

1½ cups cooked white rice, at room temperature

2 tablespoons Madeira

2 teaspoons white truffle oil

Preheat the oven to 400°F. Lightly oil a shallow baking pan.

Pull the stems from the mushroom caps. Finely chop the stems and set them aside. Season the mushroom caps all over with salt and pepper, and place them, rounded side up, in the prepared baking pan. Bake until the mushrooms are tender and starting to release their liquid, about 10 minutes. Remove them from the oven.

Meanwhile, in a large skillet, heat the olive oil over medium-high heat for 1 to 2 minutes, until it slides easily across the skillet. Add the chopped mushroom stems and sauté, stirring, until golden, about 4 minutes. Add the onion and salt and white pepper to taste and sauté, stirring occasionally, until the onion is golden, about 5 minutes more. Stir the mushroom mixture into the cooked rice along with the Madeira and truffle oil. Season the rice mixture with salt and white pepper to taste.

Turn the mushroom caps over and spoon the rice filling into the mushroom caps, pressing gently. There may be filling left over. Bake until the mushrooms are tender, about 20 minutes. Remove from the oven and let cool for 5 minutes, then arrange on a tray and serve warm.

YIELD: 20 HORS D'OEUVRES

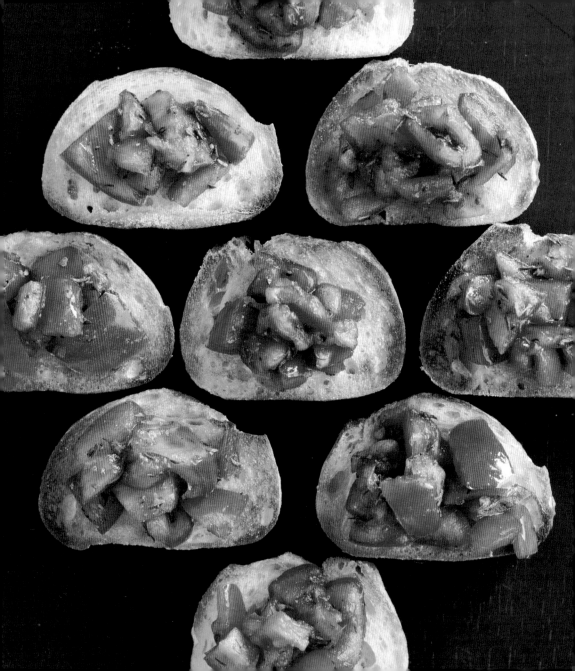

Bruschetta on a Bender

Bruschettas just wanna have fun! The vermouth here nicely lubricates this Bruschetta, electrifying the classic tomato mixture of an old party favorite.

4 medium tomatoes, peeled, seeded, and very coarsely chopped

2 teaspoons kosher salt

12 slices crusty French or Italian bread, about 3 inches in diameter

1 garlic clove, peeled and split

3 tablespoons extra-virgin olive oil

2 teaspoons balsamic vinegar

2 tablespoons dry vermouth or a fruity red wine

2 teaspoons fresh thyme leaves, or 1 teaspoon dried

1 teaspoon dried oregano

Freshly ground black pepper

Toss the tomatoes with the salt and drain for 30 minutes in a large colander set over a bowl.

Under a hot broiler, toast the bread slices on both sides. Rub the toasted top of each slice with the split garlic clove and lightly brush the top of each slice with the olive oil.

Gently press down on the drained tomatoes to extract even more juices. Then transfer them to another bowl and toss with the balsamic vinegar, dry vermouth, thyme, and oregano. Season with the pepper to taste. Spoon the tomato mixture in small mounds on top of the toasts and serve at once.

YIELD: 12 BRUSCHETTAS

Plastered Portobello Mushroom Satay

With its balsamic–dry vermouth marinade and Rosemary-Ginger Sauce infused with sherry, this satay literally translates to heaven on a stick.

MUSHROOMS:

3 large portobello mushrooms, stemmed, quartered

4 metal skewers

MARINADE:

1 garlic clove, peeled

2 tablespoons balsamic vinegar

3 tablespoons dry vermouth, port, or dry red wine

2 teaspoons brown sugar or maple syrup

¼ cup canola oil

Salt and pepper to taste

ROSEMARY-GINGER SAUCE:

½-inch piece of ginger, peeled and roughly chopped

1 jalapeño, stemmed and roughly chopped

¼ teaspoon fresh rosemary leaves

½ teaspoon fresh thyme leaves

1 tablespoon soy sauce

2 tablespoons dry sherry

3 tablespoons canola oil

Salt and pepper to taste

In a mini-processor, pulse the garlic. With the machine running, add the vinegar, dry vermouth, and brown sugar, then the oil through the feed tube. Process until smooth. Transfer to a small bowl and season with salt and pepper.

Next, in the mini-processor, place the ginger, jalapeño, rosemary, and thyme, and pulse until everything is minced. Add the soy sauce and sherry, process to blend, then add the oil and process until smooth. Transfer the mixture to a small bowl and season lightly with salt and pepper.

Heat a large grill pan or cast-iron skillet to medium high. Arrange 3 mushroom quarters horizontally on each of four metal skewers. Brush both sides of the mushrooms with the marinade. Grill the mushrooms until tender and slightly charred, occasionally brushing with any remaining marinade, about 3 to 4 minutes (6 minutes per side if using a grill pan). Sprinkle with salt and pepper.

Serve the skewers with the Rosemary-Ginger Sauce for dipping.

YIELD: 2 TO 4 SERVINGS

Coconut HELL-O! Shots

Now here's a shooting star straight from the islands that you can make any number of wishes upon! Just remember, the more of these rum shots you toss back, the more stars you'll see (or palm trees you'll be swinging from).

    1 cup water

    1 cup coconut milk

    1 (3-ounce) package Lieber's Unflavored Jel

    1 cup coconut-flavored rum

In a medium pan, combine the water and coconut milk, bringing the mixture to a boil. Mix ½ packet of Lieber's Jel into the hot water and coconut milk, and stir the mixture to dissolve. Stir in the coconut rum. Divide among eight 2-ounce paper cups. Refrigerate the cups on a serving tray after the gelatin has set and serve cold.

YIELD: 8 SHOTS

NOTE: If you don't have a nearby source for Lieber's Unflavored Jel (vegan gelatin), it's available online at VeganEssentials.com.

Fried Avocados Paint the Town

A most unusual way to treat an avocado, I know, but then there is something to be said for *experimenting*, especially when tequila is involved. To really spice things up, add a pureed chipotle pepper to the dip.

1 cup homemade vegan buttermilk (see ingredients and directions below)

1 ripe-but-still-firm avocado

1 cup all-purpose flour, plus extra for dusting

2 tablespoons tequila

½ cup panko

2 teaspoons ancho chile powder

Canola oil for deep-frying

Vegan mayonnaise for serving (such as Vegenaise) or another dipping sauce of choice

To prepare the vegan buttermilk: Blend 1 cup soy milk or other nondairy milk with 1 teaspoon lemon juice. Let the mixture stand for 10 minutes.

Halve, pit, and peel the avocado and slice it into sticks about ½-inch thick.

Arrange about ½ cup of the flour in one bowl, then combine the buttermilk and tequila in a second bowl, and mix another ½ cup of flour with the panko and chile powder in a third bowl. Dust the avocado slices with flour, dip them into buttermilk, and then into the flour/panko mixture. Quickly deep-fry them in the oil at 375°F until they are just lightly browned. Serve at once with the vegan mayonnaise or another dip of choice.

YIELD: 2 SERVINGS

Chocolate-Soused Strawberries

Holy decadence! Are you ready to pamper yourself, BIG-time? You better be, be___ ___ you ___ deserve it, and Two: This succulent treat will not take no for an answer. The ha___ ___ ___ ___ erously provided by the Frangelico is the perfect match for the chocolate and s___ ___ ___ you away from reality, one savory bite at a time. Besides, these flirtatious sweeti___ ___ ___ foreplay to *whatever* comes next.

1 pound (about 3¾ cups) fresh strawberries,
    with leaves still attached

1 pound vegan semi-sweet chocolate chips
    or chopped vegan semi-sweet chocolate

2 tablespoons chocolate almond milk
    (or vegan margarine)

1 tablespoon Frangelico, or to taste

Poke toothpicks into the tops of the strawberries.

In a double boiler, melt the vegan chocolate with the chocolate almond milk and Frangelico, stirring until smooth. Remove from heat.

One at a time, dip the strawberries into the chocolate mixture. When the chocolate sto___ ___ ___ place the strawberry on a waxed paper–lined tray. Let the strawberries cool a___ ___ ___ ready to serve.

YIELD: 3 CUPS OF CHOCOLATE-COVERED STRAWBERRIES

NOTE: If you don't have a nearby source for vegan chocolate, ___ it's available online at VeganEssentials.com.

BOOZY SOUPS

"It takes only one drink to get me drunk. The trouble is, I can't remember if it's the thirteenth or the fourteenth."

—GEORGE BURNS

HERE'S SOMETHING TO GET YOU STARTED ...

Midori Sour Patch

Sour has never been so sweet. A little vodka here, a little melon liqueur there, and a squirt of fresh lime juice all conspire to tickle your tongue with unbridled passion. Cue the afterglow!

½ cup vodka

½ cup Midori melon liqueur

¼ cup freshly squeezed lime juice

Ice

In a cocktail shaker, combine all the ingredients. Shake and strain into four martini glasses.

YIELD: 4 COCKTAILS

The Tippler's Hot + Sour Soup

People don't usually make hot and sour soup at home since it's often easier to send out for it, but as usual, making your own yields tastier results, especially Tipsy Vegan–style with wine.

½ (16-ounce) package firm tofu, cubed and pressed to remove excess water (see instructions)

1 ounce dried black mushrooms

2 ounces fresh shiitake mushrooms, chopped

4 cups vegetable stock

⅓ cup diced bamboo shoots

1 teaspoon low-sodium soy sauce

½ teaspoon sugar

1 teaspoon salt

½ teaspoon ground white pepper

2 tablespoons red wine vinegar

2 teaspoons Tabasco Sauce, or to taste

¼ cup rice wine, plus more to taste

2 tablespoons cornstarch

3 tablespoons water

½ cup mung bean sprouts

1 teaspoon toasted sesame oil

2 tablespoons thinly sliced scallions, white and light green parts only

To prepare the tofu: cube the tofu into bite-size pieces. Place a layer of paper towels on a large plate, topped with a single layer of tofu cubes. Cover the tofu with another layer of paper towels and top with another plate. Place a weight on top of the plate and drain for 1 to 2 hours.

In a medium bowl of warm water, soak the dried and fresh mushrooms for 20 minutes. After trimming off any tough stems, slice all the mushrooms.

In a large saucepan, combine the mushrooms, stock, and bamboo shoots. Bring to a boil, and simmer for 15 minutes. Stir in the soy sauce, sugar, salt, white pepper, vinegar, Tabasco Sauce, and rice wine.

In a small bowl, combine the cornstarch and water. Add a little of the hot soup to the cornstarch, and then return all to the pan. Heat to boiling, stirring. Add the tofu and bean sprouts, and cook 1 to 2 minutes. If the soup seems too thick, thin it out with more rice wine.

Before serving, turn off the heat. Mix in the sesame oil. Sprinkle each serving with scallions.

YIELD: 6 SERVINGS

High Summer Gazpacho for a Rowdy Crowd

Who better than the Tipsy Vegans of the world to rock tradition? This red wine–infused Gazpacho ignores, among other near-sacred practices, soaking bread in tomato juice—but don't worry, this recipe is still just the right amount of *thick* so as to be *oh so satisfying*, and the garnishes are especially welcomed. Note for the overachievers among us: the soup should be made on the day it's to be served; there's a lot of prep work, and the soup must be chilled for at least 2 hours before serving, so plan accordingly. Also, you will absolutely need an ample food processor.

2 large, ripe heirloom tomatoes

About a dozen rinsed basil leaves

4 cloves garlic (in all), peeled

½ to 1 cup extra-virgin olive oil

3½ pounds of late-August/early-September
　ripe plum tomatoes, about 16 to 20

3 teaspoons kosher salt

6 large bell peppers, red, yellow, and green

2 hot jalapeño, serrano, or habanero peppers
　(or to taste)

3 medium cucumbers

12 scallions

1 cup Muir Glen mixed vegetable juice or V-8 juice
　(more may be needed)

The juice and zest of 1 large smooth-skinned lime

½ cup fruity red wine (Spanish, of course)

3 to 4 tablespoons balsamic vinegar (or to taste)

5 to 6 dashes Tabasco Sauce (or to taste)

Garnishes (see below)

Chilled vodka (optional)

ROASTING THE HEIRLOOM TOMATOES:

The first step, roasting the heirloom tomatoes, may be done a day or two ahead (and you may well want to roast a lot more than two, to spread on toasted bread and serve as bruschetta with the gazpacho). Preheat the oven to 375°F. Carve an "X" in the base of each tomato and lower into rapidly boiling water for 30 seconds. Remove with a slotted spoon, let cool slightly, and slip off the skin.

Line a gratin dish, or any ovenproof dish that will hold the tomatoes snugly, with the basil leaves. Core the tomatoes and put them on the basil leaves. Scatter very thin slices of two garlic cloves over the tomatoes and pour on enough olive oil to cover one quarter of the tomatoes' height. Bake 45 to 60 minutes, until the tomatoes are soft and slightly caramelized. Set aside to bring to room temperature, or, if you're not proceeding with the recipe immediately, lift the tomatoes from the oil and refrigerate, tightly covered. Either way, keep the leftover oil, garlic, and basil leaves in a tightly covered jar and refrigerated for up to 2 weeks, during which time the oil will have myriad uses, especially in salad dressing.

ON TO THE GAZPACHO PROPER:

Take a deep breath and start prepping the vegetables. Carve an "X" in the base of each plum tomato and drop them, four at a time, into rapidly boiling water for one minute. Let them cool, slip off their skins, core and seed them (don't be too meticulous), and roughly chop. Place them in a strainer in the sink and toss them with the kosher salt. Let them drain for 20 minutes or so.

Core, seed, and roughly chop the bell peppers; do the same with the hot peppers of choice, wearing rubber gloves if you're not used to working with them. Plate the peppers and set them aside.

Peel the cucumbers, lop off the ends, cut them in half lengthwise, and scoop out the seeds with a small spoon. Cut the cucumbers into ½-inch slices. Plate them and set them aside.

Thoroughly rinse the scallions, cut off the hairy roots and any green darker than the inside of a lime. Roughly chop and set them aside.

Rev up the processor. Start with the garlic: Pulse the two remaining cloves until finely minced. Repeat with the scallions. Scrape these into the 4 to 5-quart bowl in which you will be serving the gazpacho. (If the bowl is too large for your refrigerator, you can break down the soup once it's finished into smaller containers to refrigerate, then return the soup to the cleaned bowl.)

Pulse the peppers in batches until minced, but not pureed, and stir them into the large bowl with the garlic and scallions. Do the same with the seeded cucumbers, then the plum tomatoes. Finally, pulverize the two roasted tomatoes, with 4 tablespoons of their oil.

Pour in about 1 cup of the Muir Glen vegetable juice, the juice and zest of the lime, the red wine, the balsamic vinegar, and the Tabasco Sauce. Stir thoroughly for several minutes. If it seems too thick, add more juice. If it's too thin, apply tomato paste or (*gasp!*) ketchup. Then taste very carefully. Keeping in mind that cold food tastes less salty than room temperature or warm food, salt and pepper the soup somewhat generously.

Chill the soup thoroughly, covered, for at least 2 hours. Just before serving, taste it again and add whatever you think it needs: more balsamic, more hot sauce, more red wine, more lime juice, possibly a sprinkling of sugar.

GARNISHES—OFFER AS MANY AS POSSIBLE:

- Diced seeded cucumber and finely diced red bell pepper
- Tabasco Sauce
- Chopped fresh chives
- Chopped fresh dill
- Pureed avocado (stirred in at the last minute)
- Home-made croutons

(To make croutons: Trim and cube a loaf of hearty white bread; toss cubes in a large sauté pan over medium-high heat with ample dribblings of good olive oil and, at the very end, chopped fresh herb(s) of choice, until toasty; *or* bake the oiled cubes on a sheet for 10 minutes or so at 375°F, stirring and turning halfway through.)

If the serving environment is hideously warm, you might want to float a few ice cubes in the serving bowl.

An ounce or two of chilled vodka stirred into each bowl or cup just before serving wouldn't at *all* be out of line.

YIELD: ABOUT 4 QUARTS, WHICH SHOULD SATIATE 10 TO 12 PEOPLE

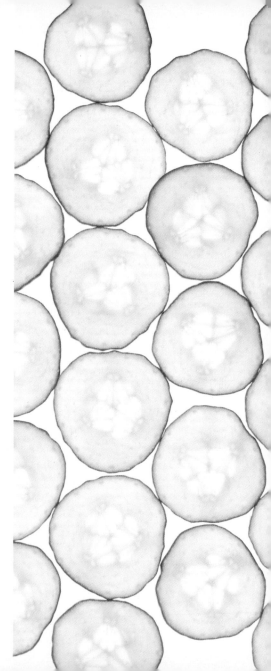

The Slurper's Kale + Potato Soup

A visually stimulating member of the cabbage family, emerald-hued kale adds rich color and a definite swagger to this recipe. Along with a hearty dose of pinot noir, garlic, onions, and carrots, the kale lets sippers and slurpers of all kinds know this isn't any old potato soup right from the very first spoonful.

2 cloves garlic, pressed

1½ cups finely chopped white onions

½ cup sliced carrots

3 tablespoons extra-virgin olive oil

1 pound Yukon Gold potatoes, peeled and cut into 1-inch pieces

4 cups vegetable stock

½ cup dry pinot noir

3 cups water

¾ pound kale, stems discarded, leaves washed thoroughly, and shredded

1 pound red potatoes, peeled or not, cut into 1-inch pieces

In a roomy saucepan, sauté the garlic, onions, and carrots in the olive oil until the vegetables are softened, about 6 minutes. Add the Yukon Gold potatoes, stock, pinot noir, and water. Bring to a boil and simmer, covered, for 10 to 15 minutes, or until the potatoes are tender.

Using an immersion blender, puree the soup, or remove the potatoes with a slotted spoon and transfer them to a blender with about 1½ cups of the cooking liquid, and puree until very smooth, then stir the mixture back into the remaining liquid. Add the kale and red potatoes and simmer until the potatoes are tender, about 12 minutes. Serve with crusty bread.

YIELD: ABOUT 8 SERVINGS

The Chugging Pumpkin Soup

Straight from the rum bottle . . . I mean, pumpkin patch, this curried soup is autumn in a bowl.

1 (4 to 5-pound) pumpkin (reserve the pumpkin
    seeds) or 2 (14-ounce) cans pumpkin puree
    (plain, not the pumpkin pie puree)

2 tablespoons extra-virgin olive oil

1 tablespoon toasted sesame oil

½ cup finely chopped shallots

5 cups vegetable stock

1 medium russet potato, peeled and chopped
    into ½-inch chunks

1 large carrot, peeled and sliced crosswise
    into ½-inch pieces

1 tablespoon dark brown sugar

2 teaspoons molasses

Finely minced zest of 1 orange

2 teaspoons curry powder

1 cup soy milk or other nondairy milk

½ cup dark rum

Dash of Tabasco Sauce

Salt and freshly ground black pepper to taste

½ teaspoon freshly grated nutmeg

1½ cups grated vegan sharp cheddar cheese,
    or nutritional yeast (optional)

To prepare the pumpkin: cut the pumpkin in half through the center and scoop out the seeds and strings. Reserve the seeds. Carefully cut away the hard peel with a paring knife—or, better, a vegetable peeler—and chop the flesh. You should have about 6 cups of pumpkin flesh.

In a large saucepan over medium-low heat, warm the olive oil with the sesame oil. Add the shallots and sauté them, stirring occasionally, until they're translucent, 3 to 4 minutes. Add the stock, pumpkin, potato, and carrot, raise the heat to high, and bring the mixture to a boil. Reduce the heat to low, cover, and simmer until the vegetables are tender, about 25 minutes.

Using an immersion blender, puree the soup until very smooth, or (carefully!) puree in batches in a blender with a towel placed over the lid. Stir in the brown sugar, molasses, orange zest, and curry powder. Over low heat, stir in the soy milk, dark rum, and Tabasco Sauce. Taste carefully. Season with salt and pepper and add the nutmeg.

Serve in warmed bowls and pass the toasted pumpkin seeds and vegan cheddar cheese for sprinkling.

YIELD: 6 SERVINGS

TOASTED PUMPKIN SEEDS (PEPITAS):

Preheat the oven to 250°F. Remove the seeds from the pumpkin(s) and pull as much of the strands and pulp away from them as you can. However, don't rinse the seeds.

In a roomy bowl, stir the seeds with peanut oil or canola oil—about a half-cup of oil for every four cups of seeds. Add a nominal amount of kosher salt. Try adding a bit of thyme, oregano, cumin, coriander, cardamom, and/or cayenne pepper, if you like.

Line baking sheet(s) with parchment paper. Spread the seeds in one layer on the sheets. Toast slowly for about an hour, checking them every 10 to 15 minutes and stirring if they're browning unevenly.

Store the toasted seeds in tightly sealed containers lined with paper towels.

Untamed Mushroom Soup

Wild mushrooms have never been so happy! Surrounded by the enticing trifecta of white wine, sherry, and Madeira, along with some classics of the veggie soup circuit, this command performance, brimming with earthy mushroom flavors, will be a primo first course dinner hit or a smashing one-act luncheon feast.

8 tablespoons (½ cup) extra-virgin olive oil

1½ cups sliced celery

¾ cup sliced shallots

¾ cup chopped onion

3 cloves garlic, pressed

3 cups sliced shiitake caps (about 6 ounces)

3 cups sliced crimini or portobello mushrooms (about 6 ounces)

3 cups sliced oyster mushrooms (about 5 ounces)

½ cup dry white wine or dry vermouth

½ cup dry sherry

¼ cup Madeira

¼ cup all-purpose flour

8 cups vegetable stock

½ cup vegan cream, such as Alpro or Soyatoo (or substitute with a smoothly blended mixture of 1 part raw cashews and 1 part water)

Salt and freshly ground black pepper to taste

In a large pot, heat 6 tablespoons of the olive oil over medium-high heat. Add the celery, shallots, onion, and garlic, and sauté until the vegetables begin to soften, about 4 minutes. Stir in the sliced mushrooms and sauté for another 5 minutes. Add the white wine, sherry, and Madeira. Boil until the liquid is reduced to a glaze, about 6 minutes.

With a small fork, mix the remaining 2 tablespoons olive oil with the flour in a small bowl until it forms a smooth paste. Add the paste to the mushroom mixture in the pot and stir until the mixture melts and lightly coats the vegetables. Gradually mix in the stock, 1 cup at a time. Bring to a boil, stirring frequently. Reduce the heat to medium low and simmer until the mushrooms are tender, stirring often, about 10 minutes. Stir in the vegan cream. Season to taste with salt and pepper.

Using an immersion blender, puree the soup until smooth. Or, if you'd rather have chunky mushroom soup, serve it as it is. Either way, serve the soup piping hot.

YIELD: 8 TO 10 SERVINGS

The Alky's Favorite Roasted Yellow Pepper Soup

When bell peppers start coming from local farms into your markets, there's not a moment to waste. First, treat yourself and splurge on the saffron, which is so worth it, especially for the luminous yellow hue and earthy gusto it imparts. Next, grab the nearest bottle of cognac, snatch up those peppers, and here's precisely what to do . . .

2 large yellow bell peppers

2 tablespoons extra-virgin olive oil

1 medium leek, white and light green parts only, thinly sliced

1 large Yukon Gold potato, peeled and cut into ½-inch cubes

4 cups vegetable stock

6 strands saffron, crumbled

1 teaspoon kosher salt

1 (14-ounce) can diced organic tomatoes, drained, preferably Muir Glen

½ cup good cognac

1 teaspoon orange zest, finely minced

Salt and freshly ground white pepper to taste

Over a burner flame or under a hot broiler, roast the yellow peppers, turning often, until they're blackened and blistered all over. Place in a plastic bag and let the peppers steam for 15 minutes. Rub off the skins with paper towels and seed and stem the peppers; do not rinse. Roughly chop the peppers and set them aside.

In a large saucepan, heat the olive oil over medium heat. Add the leeks and sauté, stirring, for 5 minutes. Add the potato cubes, stir for 1 minute, then pour in the vegetable stock. Stir in the saffron, salt, tomatoes, and cognac. Raise the heat and bring to a boil, then lower the heat and simmer for 15 minutes. Add the chopped roasted yellow peppers and simmer 5 minutes longer.

With an immersion blender, puree the mixture until very smooth. Stir in the orange zest and salt and white pepper to taste. Serve hot.

YIELD: 4 SERVINGS

STAGGERING
SALADS

"Sometimes too much to drink is barely enough."
—MARK TWAIN

HERE'S SOMETHING
TO GET YOU STARTED ...

Rum Tum Tum

This rhythmic composition of rum, Cointreau, and lime juice is *Yum Yum Yum* in your Tum Tum Tum! (Quick: say that five times fast with your mouth full.)

1 ounce white rum

½ ounce Cointreau

1 quick splash lime juice

Ice

In a cocktail shaker, combine the rum, Cointreau, lime juice, and ice and shake well. Strain into a martini glass.

YIELD: 1 COCKTAIL

Corn + Poblano Shindig Salad

This scrumptious salad is the secret to making summer last a little longer, at least during mealtime. The colorful conclave of fresh corn, peppers, tomatoes, avocados, chiles, and spices will accentuate your table as a great luncheon entrée, or a highfalutin side for evening shindigs, wine gloriously included.

STAGGERING SALADS

SALAD:

5 ears fresh corn

3 poblano peppers

16 cherry tomatoes

2 ripe avocados

2 to 3 serrano chiles (optional)

VINAIGRETTE:

3 limes, juiced

½ cup extra-virgin olive oil

2 tablespoons Marsala

1 tablespoon Dijon mustard

¼ cup chopped cilantro

Salt and freshly ground black pepper

Cut the kernels from the corn and place them in a medium glass bowl. Microwave the corn, stirring every 30 seconds, until just cooked, about 2 minutes.

Roast the poblano peppers over a gas flame or under a hot broiler, turning, until blistered all over. Place the poblanos in a paper bag and let them steam for a few minutes. When cooled, remove the stems and seeds from the poblanos and slice them into ½-inch strips.

Halve the cherry tomatoes. Halve and pit the avocados and cube the flesh. Finely chop the optional serrano peppers.

In a small bowl, whisk together the lime juice, olive oil, Marsala, mustard, cilantro, and salt and pepper to taste.

In a large bowl, toss together the corn, poblano slices, halved tomatoes, avocado cubes, and serrano peppers, if using. Toss again with the lime vinaigrette.

YIELD: 4 SERVINGS

Sunburst Salad

Break out those Jackie O's and get ready to bask in the orange glow of this salad, which will equally charm the upper-crust ladies and gentlemen who lunch for a living or a lazy afternoon gathering of family and friends on the patio. The onion, olives, and Cointreau especially give this delicious fruit salad a kick that will have your guests seeing double . . . the pleasure.

1 small Vidalia or other sweet onion, sliced into very thin rings

2 to 3 blood oranges, peeled and sliced into ¼-inch thick rounds

1 navel orange, peeled and sliced into ¼-inch thick rounds

Salt and freshly ground white pepper to taste

2 to 3 tablespoons freshly squeezed orange juice

2 tablespoons Cointreau

8 black Kalamata olives, pitted and halved

2 tablespoons extra-virgin olive oil

Pack the onion rings into a bowl, cover with ice, and fill the bowl with cold water. Refrigerate for 30 minutes.

When you're about ready to serve the salad, fan the orange rings in rows on a large plate, alternating blood and navel orange slices. Drain the onions, pat them dry with paper towels, and tuck the onion rings in among the orange slices. Lightly dust the orange and onion rings with salt and white pepper.

Drizzle the salad with the orange juice and Cointreau, scatter the olives over all, and sprinkle with the olive oil.

YIELD: 3 TO 4 SERVINGS

Macho Mâche Salad with Toasted Coconut, Nuts + Oranges

The fluffy mâche, a fancy handle for mild lettuce-flavored greens, offers the perfect contrasting texture for the brawny nuts and orange sections, which are all the more empowered by the orange and red wine vinaigrette. And for the island child inside each of us, coconut makes a most welcomed appearance!

SALAD:

¼ cup sweetened coconut

¼ cup Spanish peanuts

¼ cup pine nuts

1 orange, peeled and cut into sections, any seeds discarded

3 cups mâche (or Boston or Romaine lettuce), rinsed and spun dry

VINAIGRETTE:

3 tablespoons freshly squeezed orange juice

1 tablespoon red wine vinegar

2 tablespoons good dry red wine

1 teaspoon fresh thyme leaves, minced, or ½ teaspoon dried thyme

½ teaspoon kosher salt

½ teaspoon freshly ground black pepper

¼ cup extra-virgin olive oil

In a medium skillet, lightly toast the coconut, peanuts, and pine nuts over medium-low heat just until the coconut starts to take on some color, about 2 to 3 minutes. In a roomy bowl, combine the coconut mixture with the orange sections and mâche.

In a medium bowl, combine the orange juice, vinegar, red wine, thyme, salt, and pepper, then whisk in the olive oil in a steady stream to emulsify. Toss the salad with the vinaigrette and serve.

YIELD: 2 AMPLE SERVINGS

Mandarin Orange + Red Onion Salad with a Toast of Champagne

Get ready for the urge to throw confetti and kiss everyone in sight every time you serve this champagne-drenched salad bursting with festive colors to feed the heart and the soul. "New Year's Resolution: Have more fun!" can now be checked off your list.

DRESSING:

¼ cup balsamic vinegar

Zest of 1 orange

1 tablespoon brown sugar

½ teaspoon salt

¼ teaspoon freshly ground black pepper

¾ cup extra-virgin olive oil

SALAD:

1 small red onion, thinly sliced

1 large head (or 2 small heads) endive, wiped with a moist cloth (do not rinse)

1 large head red leaf lettuce, torn into bite-size pieces (if unavailable, then double the amount of radicchio below)

1 medium head radicchio, torn into bite-size pieces

2 (12-ounce) cans mandarin oranges, drained

½ cup dried cranberries

½ cup good champagne

In a medium bowl, whisk together the vinegar, zest, brown sugar, salt, and pepper. Whisk in the oil gradually.

About 30 minutes before serving, in a small bowl, toss the red onion with 2 tablespoons of the dressing. Cover and set aside.

Cut the endive crosswise into ½-inch wide pieces. Separate the pieces into strips, discarding any tough, solid, center pieces.

When ready to serve, in a large bowl, toss the lettuces and endive with the remaining dressing. Top each portion with orange segments and red onions, then sprinkle with the cranberries. Pour the champagne over the salad, toss again, and serve.

YIELD: 6 TO 8 SERVINGS

Sparkling Fruit Cocktail

R.I.P., boring old fruit salad! Served in tall glasses, made-to-order, and dressed to the hilt in champagne, this sun-kissed concoction effortlessly flows from day to evening, working as a bubbly appetizer, salad course, or dessert. Quantities of the ingredients can easily be adjusted to accommodate the number of people you're aiming to please. Of course, adding extra champagne is always an option, and *highly* recommended.

3 ripe peaches, peeled, pitted, and sliced

18 seedless green grapes, halved

1 ripe cantaloupe, scooped into small balls with melon baller

1 pint strawberries, stemmed and halved

1 bottle chilled champagne

In a large bowl, combine the peach slices, grape halves, cantaloupe balls, and halved strawberries and toss them together well. Transfer the fruit to 14-ounce drinking glasses until each glass is half filled. Thoroughly chill the fruit and the glasses.

Just before serving, fill the glasses with the champagne. Each guest can drink the champagne with dinner, then eat the fruit with a long spoon for dessert.

YIELD: 4 SERVINGS

Balmy Bell Peppers with Golden Raisins + Arugula

Close your eyes for a moment and imagine steeping golden raisins in warm cognac, turning them into irresistibly sweet nuggets bursting with the distinct flavor that only the world's most famous brandy can conjure. Now, imagine adding some sautéed peppers, fennel, balsamic vinegar, and arugula. Let yourself get carried away with the pure ecstasy that awaits you and your guests with every bite of this salad.

½ cup golden raisins

¾ cup cognac

3 tablespoons extra-virgin olive oil

1 large red bell pepper, sliced into ¼-inch strips

1 large yellow bell pepper, sliced into ¼-inch strips

1 large orange bell pepper, sliced into ¼-inch strips

2 teaspoons fennel seeds

1 tablespoon balsamic vinegar

Salt and freshly ground black pepper to taste

4 cups baby arugula leaves

In a 1-cup glass measure, place the raisins and cover them with the cognac. Microwave the raisins until the cognac bubbles lightly, about 1 minute. Let the raisins steep for 20 minutes.

In a large, heavy skillet, heat the oil over medium-high heat. Add all the peppers and sauté until slightly softened, stirring occasionally, about 7 minutes. Add the raisins and fennel seeds and continue to cook until the peppers are soft, about 5 minutes. Stir in the vinegar and season with salt and pepper.

When you're ready to serve, add the arugula to the peppers and stir until the arugula begins to wilt, about 1 minute. Divide the mixture among two to four plates and serve.

YIELD: 2 TO 4 SERVINGS

Wild Rice Under the Influence

All you untamed rum lovers (you know who you are!), really get your rum on by bringing the Polynesian flare of this rice salad to your next bash.

SALAD:

2 cups vegetable stock

½ cup wild rice

½ cup white rice

1 cup snow peas, sliced in half crosswise

1 red bell pepper, cored, seeded, and diced

¾ cup diced celery

⅔ cup sliced water chestnuts

½ cup canned mandarin oranges, drained

2 scallions, chopped

DRESSING:

3 tablespoons freshly squeezed orange juice

2 teaspoons orange zest

¼ cup white rum

2 teaspoons sugar

1 teaspoon soy sauce

1 teaspoon canola oil

½ teaspoon toasted sesame oil

½ teaspoon fresh lemon juice

1 smallish clove garlic, pressed

1 teaspoon grated fresh ginger

In a medium saucepan, bring the stock to a boil. Add both the wild and white rice. Cover, reduce to medium heat, and simmer for 15 to 20 minutes, or until the rice is tender and the liquid is absorbed. Rinse the rice with cold water, drain it well, and place it in a medium bowl.

In a saucepan of boiling water, blanch the snow peas for 1 to 2 minutes, or until tender-crisp. Immediately transfer the snow peas to a bowl of ice water to stop the cooking and retain the bright green color. Drain well. Add the snow peas to the rice along with the red bell peppers, celery, water chestnuts, mandarin oranges, and scallions. Toss thoroughly.

In a small bowl, whisk together all the dressing ingredients.

Pour the dressing over the salad and toss well.

YIELD: 4 SERVINGS

Reveling Red Cabbage, Apple + Walnut Salad

A tasty mélange of flavors and textures, this sherry-infused salad could start, accompany, or even punctuate a meal, or become a refreshing *private* lunch for two romantic revelers (I won't tell, if you don't!).

¼ head red cabbage

1 tablespoon sherry vinegar

2 tablespoons dry sherry

2 tablespoons walnut oil

1 tablespoon red currant jelly

1 teaspoon sugar

1 Golden Delicious apple

½ teaspoon fresh lemon juice

½ cup toasted walnuts

Salt and pepper

Using a mandoline or V-slicer, thinly shred the red cabbage. In a medium bowl, whisk the sherry vinegar and the sherry with the walnut oil, red currant jelly, and sugar. Toss the cabbage with the vinegar mixture.

Peel the apple and slice it into thin discs on the mandoline. Cover the floor of a plate with the apple slices and sprinkle them lightly with the lemon juice to prevent discoloration. Top with the red cabbage salad and sprinkle with walnuts. Season to taste with salt and pepper.

YIELD: 2 TO 3 SERVINGS

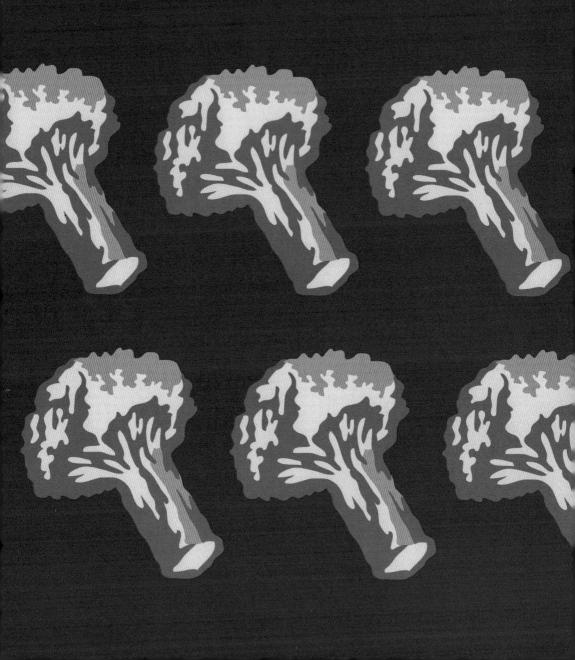

THE GUZZLER'S GARDEN OF SIDE DISHES

4

"When I read about the evils of drinking, I gave up reading."

—HENNY YOUNGMAN

HERE'S SOMETHING
TO GET YOU STARTED ...

Wino Cool-Aid

Whether poolside, beach-bound, or just dreaming you are, pucker up and get ready for long, cool kisses from this citric elixir. It'll refresh you on those steamy hot days and make visions of sunshine and mischief dance in your head any time of year. Just make sure all the ingredients are very cold, for the full, icy-licious effect.

¼ cup grapefruit juice

¼ cup pineapple juice

¼ cup lime juice

¼ cup lemon juice

2 cups good Chablis

3 cups lemon-lime soda, such as 7-Up

In a pitcher, mix the grapefruit, pineapple, lime, and lemon juices.

Divide the Chablis among four tall wine glasses and top with the lemon-lime soda. Stir in the juice mixture and serve at once.

YIELD: 4 SERVINGS

Hey, Baby! Artichokes

Native to the Mediterranean, artichokes have become an exotic standard at dinners, festive parties, or for indulgent snacks. For this incarnation, artichokes tango with white wine and spices for a mouthy fête!

4 baby artichokes, about 2 ounces each

Juice of ½ lemon, other half of lemon reserved for rubbing the artichokes

Juice of ½ lime, other half of lime reserved for rubbing the artichokes

½ cup vegetable stock

½ cup dry white wine

¼ cup extra-virgin olive oil

Garlic powder to taste

¼ teaspoon coriander seeds

¼ teaspoon crushed cardamom pods

1 teaspoon mustard seeds

Kosher salt to taste

2 teaspoons whole-grain mustard

About ½ cup vegan mayonnaise, such as Vegenaise

Remove the round bottom leaves from the artichokes, trim the leaf tips, and cut them in half lengthwise. Remove any outer leaves that seem hard and sharp, and any inner leaves that have crimson edges. Rub the cut surfaces of the reserved halves of the lemon and lime over the outer surfaces of the artichokes.

In a roomy microwavable casserole dish, combine the artichokes, lemon and lime juices, stock, white wine, oil, garlic powder, spices, and salt to taste. Cover tightly with plastic wrap. Microwave on high for 7 minutes.

Remove from the microwave. Uncover, test the artichokes for doneness (a skewer should go through an artichoke easily), and turn the artichokes over. Re-cover and cook for 2 to 3 minutes longer.

Remove from the microwave. Pierce the plastic with a sharp knife. Let the artichokes stand, covered, until cool.

Stir about ½ cup of the braising liquid and the whole-grain mustard into the vegan mayonnaise and serve as a dip for the artichoke leaves. Or, serve the artichokes with another dipping sauce of choice.

YIELD: 2 SERVINGS

Buxom Broccoli Sesame

The full-figured broccoli gets the royal (and boozy) treatment here, tossed in a spirited fusion of spices and vermouth. The green buds and sesame seeds have a natural flavor affinity for each other, while the orange zest and Cointreau supply the exclamation point for this inebriated creation.

1 medium head broccoli

2 teaspoons sesame seeds

1 teaspoon toasted sesame oil

2 tablespoons extra-virgin olive oil

2½ tablespoons thinly sliced cloves garlic

½ teaspoon red pepper flakes

½ teaspoon salt

¼ cup dry vermouth or rice wine

1 tablespoon soy sauce

½ teaspoon finely grated orange peel

Cointreau, for final drizzling

Rinse the broccoli. Carve it into florets about 3-inches long. Cut the thick stems into ¼-inch coins. There should be about 7 cups of broccoli.

In a small skillet, toast the sesame seeds until golden, about 5 minutes, shaking the skillet often. Transfer to a small bowl.

In another small skillet, place the sesame oil, olive oil, and garlic slivers over low heat. Sauté the garlic, stirring frequently, until it's nicely toasted to a deep golden brown, about 6 minutes. Add the pepper flakes to the hot oil and stir. Scrape the garlic mixture into another small bowl.

In the same skillet, toss the broccoli, salt, and vermouth. Cover the pan and set it over high heat. Cook until the broccoli is tender, shaking the pan often and stirring once, about 4 minutes. Uncover the skillet (the liquid should be gone) and toss. Stir in the garlic mixture, soy sauce, and orange peel. Transfer to a warm serving platter, sprinkle with sesame seeds, and drizzle with Cointreau to taste.

YIELD: 4 SERVINGS

Splish Splash Pepper-Roasted Cauliflower

Brassica oleracea botrytis's days of being the shy, bland wallflower on the vegetable circuit are over. With the help of a stunner named sherry and a splash splash of fiery pepper-flavored vodka, this cauliflower dish becomes the life of the party!

¼ cup low-sodium soy sauce

2 to 3 tablespoons dry sherry

2 tablespoons canola oil

1 teaspoon coarsely ground black pepper

1 teaspoon sugar

1 large head cauliflower, cut into smallish, evenly sized florets

1 medium jalapeño, finely chopped (optional; taste for heat level before using!)

Pepper-flavored vodka

THE GUZZLER'S GARDEN OF SIDE DISHES

Preheat the oven to 450°F and place a rack in the middle. In a large bowl, stir together the soy sauce, sherry, oil, pepper, and sugar. Add the cauliflower florets and toss to coat. Let the cauliflower marinate for 20 minutes, tossing occasionally.

On a large, parchment-lined baking sheet, arrange the cauliflower in a single layer. Sprinkle the optional jalapeño over the cauliflower before roasting (or after roasting, if you don't mind the crunch). Roast until tender and slightly blackened, about 20 minutes. Serve hot or at room temperature, splashed lightly with the vodka.

YIELD: 2 TO 4 SERVINGS

The Guzzler's Green Beans + Yellow Peppers with Currants

While white wine is *always* in season, this easy side dish is best served in late summer and early autumn, when green beans are mature and bursting with flavor, and local bell peppers are at their most plentiful.

1 pound green beans, trimmed and sliced into
    1-inch pieces

2 large yellow peppers

4 tablespoons extra-virgin olive oil

1 tablespoon currants

2 tablespoons diced pimientos

Generous pinch of kosher salt

8 grates nutmeg

2 teaspoons soy sauce

2 tablespoons dry white wine

Sea salt

In 5 quarts of well-salted boiling water, cook the beans until tender-crisp, 4 to 7 minutes, tasting for texture regularly after 4 minutes. When they're just right, drain the beans immediately and plunge them into a bowl of ice water to stop cooking. Drain them well.

Peel the yellow peppers by cutting off the stem ends and discarding them along with the seeds. Carve the peppers into segments by slicing along their crevices. Then, with a swivel-peeler, use light sawing motions to peel the skin from the peppers. Slice them into 1 x ½-inch pieces.

Pour 2 tablespoons of the olive oil into a large preheated skillet over medium-high heat. Add the peppers—they should sizzle when they hit the oil—and sauté, stirring often, for about 10 minutes, just until the peppers begin to brown. Add the currants, pimientos, salt, nutmeg, soy sauce, and white wine and stir, still over lively heat, for a few moments.

Add the cooked beans and the remaining olive oil and stir until the beans are heated through.

Serve at once, flecked with sea salt.

YIELD: 2 AMPLE SERVINGS

Okra, Pepper + Tomato Hullabaloo

Okay, people, for those of you who say you don't like okra because of the slimy texture, your days of lamenting are over. Using small okra and cooking for just 6 to 7 minutes completely avoids the issues that stem from overcooking. Oh, and did I mention okra's tipsy costar in our little production here: tall, dark, and handsome rum! It's time to give okra a second chance at love, my friends.

2 tablespoons canola oil

1 medium onion, diced

2 poblano peppers, stemmed, seeded, and sliced into ¼-inch strips

2 cups small okra, the size of your little finger, trimmed (about ½ pound)

½ teaspoon kosher salt, or more to taste

¼ teaspoon freshly ground black pepper

2 large ripe tomatoes, peeled your way, stemmed, seeded, squeezed,
     and chopped into ½-inch pieces

¼ cup dark rum

In a large skillet, heat the canola oil over medium heat. Add the onion and cook, stirring, for 5 minutes. Add the poblano strips, okra, salt, and pepper and cook, stirring frequently, for 3 minutes. Toss in the tomatoes and turn the heat to low. Splash on the rum and cook, partially covered, just until the tomatoes are heated through, 3 to 4 minutes. Carefully taste for seasoning and adjust if needed. Serve warm.

YIELD: 2 AMPLE SERVINGS

Oh Snap! Stir-Fried Sugar Snap Peas

Medium-dry sherry combines well with the soy sauce and smoked paprika to make a delicious addition to a sauce that really wakes up the sugar snap peas. In other words, when these sweeties come into season, lunge for them and this recipe!

THE GUZZLER'S GARDEN OF SIDE DISHES

2 tablespoons soy sauce

3 tablespoons medium-dry sherry

2 teaspoons cornstarch

1 teaspoon sugar, or slightly more if the peas
    aren't very sweet

1 teaspoon smoked paprika

½ teaspoon kosher salt

2 tablespoons extra-virgin olive oil

3 cloves garlic, minced

¼ cup finely minced peeled fresh ginger

1 pound sugar snap peas, trimmed

¾ cup water

2 bunches scallions (white and pale green parts only),
    cut into ¾-inch pieces

Freshly ground black pepper to taste

In a small bowl, stir together the soy sauce, sherry, cornstarch, sugar, paprika, and salt.

Heat a large wok or heavy skillet over high heat. Add the olive oil, and when it is hot but not smoking, stir-fry the garlic and ginger for about 30 seconds.

Add the sugar snap peas and stir-fry for 1 minute. Add the water and boil, stirring occasionally, until the peas are just crisp-tender, 1 to 2 minutes.

Stir the soy sauce mixture again and pour it over the peas. Add the scallions. Boil, stirring, until the sauce is thickened and no longer cloudy, about 2 minutes. Season to taste with the pepper.

YIELD: 4 SERVINGS

Rice + Pasta Pilaf Gets Lit with Scallions + Garlic

Forget everything you know about pilaf, because Riesling has its own come-hither plans for this normally reserved rice and pasta dish.

2 tablespoons extra-virgin olive oil

1 ounce or so dried angel-hair pasta, broken into small pieces to make about ½ cup

1 cup basmati rice

4 scallions, light green and white parts only, minced

2 cloves garlic, pressed

1 cup water

1 cup dry Riesling

1 teaspoon salt

In a 3-quart saucepan, heat the oil over medium-high heat until hot but not smoking. Sauté the pasta, stirring constantly, until browned, 3 to 4 minutes. Add the rice and sauté, stirring, until coated with oil. Stir in the scallions and garlic, and cook, still stirring, for about 1 minute.

Add the water, Riesling, and salt and bring to a boil. Reduce the heat to low and cook, covered, until the liquid is absorbed, about 15 minutes. Remove from the heat, fluff with a fork, then let the rice stand, covered, for 5 minutes.

YIELD: 4 SERVINGS

Rockin' Roasted Potatoes with Racy Rosemary + Mustard

These rousing spuds start out looking wet and wild (which under some circumstances can be a very hot bonus—*wink, wink!*), but the mixture with vodka and vermouth cooks down to leave the potatoes crispy, crusty, and tangy, just how you'll want them again and again.

⅓ cup plus 1 tablespoon Dijon mustard

⅓ cup extra-virgin olive oil

2 tablespoons vodka

1 tablespoon dry vermouth or dry white wine

1 tablespoon bottled horseradish

2 cloves garlic, pressed

1 teaspoon smoked paprika

1 tablespoon chopped fresh rosemary leaves

1 teaspoon kosher salt

Pepper to taste

1 teaspoon caraway seeds

½ teaspoon cayenne pepper

1 teaspoon red pepper flakes

2 pounds red-skinned and Yukon Gold potatoes, cut into ¾- to 1-inch chunks

Preheat the oven to 400°F. Line a large rimmed baking sheet with parchment paper.

In a large bowl, whisk together the mustard, olive oil, vodka, vermouth, horseradish, garlic, paprika, rosemary, salt, pepper, caraway seeds, cayenne, and pepper flakes. Add the potatoes and toss with your hands to coat. Dump the potatoes onto the prepared baking sheet and spread them out in a single layer. Roast, tossing with a spatula a few times, until the potatoes are crusty on the outside and tender throughout, 50 to 55 minutes.

YIELD: 4 SERVINGS

Cocky Coconut Rice

While always perfect for dressing up your favorite curry creations or Indonesian vegetable dishes, this vermouth-infused coconut rice can be a bold and unexpected surprise anytime, whether island hopping or channel-surfing.

1½ cups long-grain rice

2 cups coconut milk

½ cup dry vermouth or dry white wine

½ teaspoon salt

2 bay leaves

2 curry leaves (optional)

In a heavy saucepan, bring the ingredients to a boil. Lower heat and simmer, covered, for 20 minutes. Remove from heat and let stand, covered, until ready to serve. Remove and discard bay and curry leaves before serving.

YIELD: 4 TO 6 SERVINGS

Swigs of Spinach with Ground Red Chile + Sesame Seeds

Korean in origin, adding a jalapeño and a few swigs of pepper-flavored vodka to this spinach spectacular makes it all the sassier.

1 tablespoon white vinegar

2½ pounds spinach, heavy stems removed

2 tablespoons pepper-flavored vodka

1 large clove garlic, finely chopped

1 scallion, white and light green parts only, finely chopped

1 jalapeño, seeded and finely chopped

2½ teaspoons toasted sesame seeds

2 tablespoons soy sauce

1 tablespoon toasted sesame oil

2 teaspoons ground Korean red chile, or 1 teaspoon cayenne pepper

¼ teaspoon salt

Bring a large saucepan of water to a boil with the vinegar, then plunge the spinach into the water for 10 seconds and drain in a colander. Immediately run cold water over the spinach to stop it from cooking any further. Squeeze the water out of the spinach by pressing it firmly against the holes in the colander with the back of a spoon, then dry further by pressing with paper towels. Chop very coarsely.

In a large bowl, mix together the vodka, garlic, scallion, jalapeño, sesame seeds, soy sauce, sesame oil, ½ teaspoon of the ground chile, and salt. Add the spinach and mix well. Transfer to a serving platter and garnish with the remaining ground chile. Serve at room temperature.

YIELD: 3 TO 4 SERVINGS

Sweet-and-Sour Oktoberfest Cabbage

With a distinct German accent (i.e., beer!), this Sweet-and-Sour Cabbage will help you bring a tasty touch of Oktoberfest to any occasion. While accordions, yodeling, and wooden clogs are optional, playing dress-up can be fun.

2 tablespoons extra-virgin olive oil

2 tablespoons canola oil

2 large yellow onions, peeled and coarsely chopped

¼ cup vegetable stock

¼ cup light beer of choice

1 large red cabbage, about 2½ pounds, trimmed, cut into eighths,
    then each eighth sliced crosswise, ½-inch thick

¾ pound carrots, peeled and coarsely shredded

1½ tablespoons sugar

1 teaspoon salt

¼ teaspoon freshly ground black pepper

¾ cup cider vinegar

In a heavy 12-inch skillet, heat the olive oil and canola oil over moderate heat for 1 minute. Add the onions and sauté for 10 minutes, stirring often, until lightly browned. Add the stock and beer and pile the cabbage into the skillet. Reduce the heat to low, cover tightly, and steam for 20 minutes. Pile the carrots on top of the cabbage, re-cover, and steam for 20 minutes longer.

Sprinkle with the sugar, salt, and pepper, then pour in the vinegar and toss gently but thoroughly. Raise the heat to moderate and boil, uncovered, stirring occasionally, for 3 to 5 minutes, just until the skillet juices reduce a little. Taste for salt and adjust as needed. Serve at once.

YIELD: 6 SERVINGS

Blitzed Brussels Sprouts Moutarde

Don't let the fancy name fool you: Brussels Sprouts Moutarde is particularly useful when the oven and stovetop are busy, because it can be prepared entirely in a microwave oven (but that will be our little secret). Also, halving the sprouts allows them to drink-up all the spry flavors of the mustard sauce, especially the vermouth and cognac. If you need to double this for a holiday feast or those unexpected dinner guests, there'll be time to microwave it in two batches, especially if you're serving buffet-style.

5 tablespoons unsalted vegan margarine

3 tablespoons smooth Dijon mustard

2 teaspoons dried tarragon (or thyme, if you don't like tarragon)

2 teaspoons freshly squeezed lemon juice

1 teaspoon lemon zest

½ teaspoon vanilla extract

½ cup vegetable stock

1 teaspoon balsamic vinegar

3 good splashes of dry vermouth or dry white wine

2 tablespoons cognac

2 pounds Brussels sprouts, rinsed, trimmed, and halved lengthwise

Place the margarine in a large microwave-proof casserole and cover with a not-too-tight-fitting lid. Microwave on full power for 1 minute, or until the margarine is melted. Stir in everything else, adding the sprouts last. Mix well and return the lid.

Microwave on full power for 4 to 9 minutes, depending on your wattage and your preference for al dente Brussels sprouts. Start testing and stirring at 4 minutes, anyway.

YIELD: 4 TO 6 SERVINGS

Whoop It Up! Balsamic Zucchini

Balsamic vinegar and Madeira work together to broaden the tepid flavor of this popular summer squash with a funny name. Because this zesty zucchini dish is served at room temperature, it can be made ahead of time and set aside for a good half-hour, allowing you to get a head-start on cocktails before your guests arrive.

 2 pounds medium zucchini, cut diagonally into ¾-inch thick slices

 3 tablespoons extra-virgin olive oil

 ½ teaspoon salt

 ½ teaspoon coarsely ground black pepper

 2 tablespoons balsamic vinegar

 2 tablespoons Madeira

 ⅓ cup freshly grated vegan Parmesan cheese, or nutritional yeast (optional)

 ¼ cup pine nuts, toasted and finely chopped

Heat the broiler. In a medium bowl, toss the zucchini with the oil, salt, and pepper. On a baking sheet lined with foil or parchment paper, arrange the zucchini in one layer. Broil the zucchini 3 to 5 inches from the heat source, without turning, until it's browned in spots and beginning to soften, 4 to 6 minutes.

Drizzle the vinegar and Madeira over the zucchini and shake the pan a few times, then continue to broil until most of the liquid is evaporated, about 3 minutes. If desired, sprinkle the vegan Parmesan cheese over the zucchini and broil about 1 minute longer. Cool to room temperature and serve sprinkled with the pine nuts.

YIELD: 2 AMPLE SERVINGS

High-Octane Balsamic Mushrooms

These autumnal mushrooms are braced considerably by the addition of the iconic Angostura Aromatic Bitters. High in alcohol content (!!!), this near-magical ingredient has a bitter flavor, hence the name and its talent for reviving even the lamest taste buds.

1 tablespoon balsamic vinegar

2 teaspoons Angostura Aromatic Bitters

2 teaspoons dark brown sugar

1 tablespoon water

4 tablespoons extra-virgin olive oil

1 pound cremini mushrooms, wiped clean and quartered

¾ teaspoon kosher salt

2 cloves garlic, pressed

Freshly ground black pepper

In a small dish, combine the balsamic vinegar, bitters, brown sugar, and water and set near the stove.

In a 10-inch, straight-sided stainless steel pan, heat 3 tablespoons of the olive oil over medium-high heat. When the oil is hot, add the mushrooms and salt, and immediately stir with a wooden spoon until the mushrooms have absorbed all the oil.

Let the mushrooms cook undisturbed for 2 minutes, and then stir once. The pan will look dry, but keep the heat at medium high and continue to cook, stirring infrequently, until the mushrooms have given up their liquid and are shrunken, glistening, and taking on some deep orange-brown color, 6 to 7 minutes more (the bottom of the pan will be brown).

Turn the heat to low, add the garlic and the remaining tablespoon of olive oil, and cook, stirring, until the garlic is fragrant, 15 to 20 seconds. Carefully add the balsamic mixture and cook, stirring, until the liquid reduces to a glazy consistency that coats the mushrooms, 15 to 20 seconds. Season with a few grinds of the pepper.

Immediately transfer the mushrooms to a serving dish, using a rubber spatula to scrape out all of the garlicky sauce. Let the mushrooms sit for a few minutes and then serve warm.

YIELD: 4 SERVINGS

THE GUZZLER'S GARDEN OF SIDE DISHES

Pampered Asparagus with Vegenaise Verte

A descendent of the illustrious lily family, and boasting such famed cousins as onions and garlic, here asparagus brings its tasty lineage to your buffet with its new favorite sidekick, a smooth, Cointreau-infused dipping sauce. But, first, be sure to pamper your asparagus by soaking the thick, peeled stalks in lightly sugared water before roasting them in a very hot oven, which helps to caramelize them to perfection.

1½ pounds thick asparagus, dry ends snapped off and stalks peeled

2 to 3 tablespoons sugar

5 tablespoons extra-virgin olive oil

Sea salt and freshly ground black pepper

½ cup packed Italian parsley leaves (no stems)

1 tablespoon lime juice

1 teaspoon smooth Dijon mustard, Maille preferred

½ cup vegan mayonnaise, such as Vegenaise

¼ cup vegan sour cream

2 tablespoons Cointreau

1 pinch dried tarragon

½ teaspoon orange zest

Smoked paprika, for sprinkling the vegan mayonnaise (optional)

Soak the peeled asparagus for 1 to 2 hours in a few quarts of cool water with 2 to 3 tablespoons of sugar dissolved in it.

Preheat the oven to 425°F. Arrange the asparagus in one layer on a foil-lined jelly roll pan. Drizzle with 3 tablespoons of the olive oil and roll the spears to coat them. Sprinkle judiciously with salt and pepper. Roast the asparagus for 15 to 20 minutes, until just tender.

In the container of a standing blender, place the parsley, the remaining 2 tablespoons of olive oil, lime juice, mustard, vegan mayonnaise, vegan sour cream, Cointreau, tarragon, and orange zest. Puree the ingredients, scraping down the sides of the container with a rubber spatula several times. Taste for salt and pepper. Stir well.

Serve the asparagus hot, warm, or at room temperature with the vegan mayonnaise mixture in individual ramekins, sprinkled with the optional paprika.

YIELD: 3 TO 4 SIDE-DISH SERVINGS, 5 TO 6 APPETIZER PORTIONS

BRUNCH BUZZ

5

"I feel sorry for people who don't drink. When they wake up in the morning, that's as good as they're going to feel all day."
—FRANK SINATRA

HERE'S SOMETHING TO GET YOU STARTED ...

Brunch Broad Mimosa

This fluted broad is classed-up even more when it meets the newest neighbor in Brunch Town: Cointreau.

½ navel orange

Lemon wedge

Cold champagne

1 ounce Cointreau

Place two ice cubes in a large chilled wine glass. Squeeze the orange half and lemon wedge over the ice, nearly fill the glass with the champagne, and finish with the Cointreau. Stir well and serve.

YIELD: 1 MIMOSA

Bloody Queen Mary

You may think you know her, but everything you ever thought is about to be turned on its head. Warning: this one is not for sissies! Now proceed . . .

2½ cups chilled vodka

½ cup chopped onion

2 small cloves garlic, pressed with a garlic press

2 small jalapeños, stemmed, seeded, and coarsely chopped (or to taste)

1 habanero or Scotch bonnet chile pepper, stemmed, seeded, and coarsely chopped (or to taste); wear rubber gloves if you are not used to working with hot peppers

1 medium red bell pepper, stemmed, seeded, and coarsely chopped

2 tablespoons Tabasco Sauce or other hot sauce of choice (or to taste)

5 cups tomato or V-8 juice

3 tablespoons freshly grated horseradish

2 tablespoons freshly squeezed lemon juice

2 teaspoons celery salt

1 teaspoon freshly ground black pepper

Lime wedges and celery ribs, for serving

In a standing blender, combine the vodka with the onion, garlic, the jalapeños, habanero and bell peppers, and hot sauce. Puree the mixture until smooth.

In a large pitcher (at least ½ gallon), combine the vodka mixture with the tomato juice, horseradish, lemon juice, celery salt, and pepper and stir vigorously to blend. Strain (or just pour) into ice-filled tall glasses and serve with the lime wedges and celery ribs.

YIELD: 6 TO 8 DRINKS

BRUNCH BUZZ

Party Monster Pancakes

Should you find yourself doing the walk of shame or merely stumbling in the door at the crack of dawn, these airy pancakes will be a welcome sight. While always a brunch favorite, especially after an all-nighter, let's face it, with cinnamon, bananas, vanilla, walnuts, and the secret ingredient, amaretto, they're really soothing anytime, day or night.

1½ cups all-purpose flour	3 medium very ripe bananas, mashed with a fork
1½ teaspoons baking powder	1 teaspoon vanilla extract
½ teaspoon baking soda	1 tablespoon amaretto
Pinch of salt	½ cup chopped toasted walnuts
¼ teaspoon cinnamon	1 tablespoon canola oil, plus additional
1½ cups soy milk or other nondairy milk	Additional bananas for slicing and serving
1 teaspoon white vinegar	Maple syrup for serving

In a large bowl, sift the flour with the baking powder, baking soda, salt, and cinnamon.

In a separate large bowl, stir the soy milk with the vinegar and let the mixture rest for 5 minutes. Stir in the mashed bananas, vanilla, and amaretto, then pour the mixture into the flour mixture without over-blending. Fold in the walnuts.

In a large nonstick skillet, heat the canola oil until it slides easily across the pan. Pour ¼ cup of the batter per pancake into the hot skillet and cook until bubbles appear on the surface, 1 to 2 minutes. Flip the pancakes with a spatula and cook 1 to 2 minutes more, until golden brown on both sides. Transfer to a large plate and cover loosely with foil to keep warm. Continue making pancakes, brushing the skillet with oil for each batch.

Serve with sliced bananas and maple syrup.

YIELD: 8 TO 10 MEDIUM PANCAKES

The Hangover Tofu Omelet
with Sautéed Chopped Bell Pepper Filling

Following an unbridled marathon of revelry and laughter, your weekend guests will be happily red-eyed with gratitude when you spring this masterpiece of an omelet on them at the brunch table. And if you haven't yet discovered nutritional yeast, get ready to fall in love. Not to be confused with baking yeast or brewer's yeast, this humble flake imparts a deliciously cheesy, nutty flavor.

3 tablespoons extra-virgin olive oil

1 red bell pepper, stemmed, seeded, and diced

6 ounces extra-firm silken tofu, cubed and pressed to remove excess water (see instructions on page 31)

1 tablespoon soy milk or other nondairy milk

1 tablespoon Marsala

1 tablespoon powdered nutritional yeast

1 tablespoon cornstarch

1 teaspoon tahini

1 to 2 pinches onion powder

1 to 2 pinches garlic powder

⅛ teaspoon turmeric

Salt and freshly ground black pepper to taste

1 pinch smoked paprika

In a medium skillet over medium-high heat, place 1 tablespoon of the olive oil. Add the bell pepper and sauté until softened and beginning to brown, about 5 minutes.

In a blender, combine the tofu, soy milk, Marsala, yeast, cornstarch, tahini, onion and garlic powders, turmeric, salt, pepper, and paprika. Blend until smooth.

In another large nonstick skillet over medium-high heat, place the remaining 2 tablespoons of olive oil. When the oil slides easily across the skillet when tilted, pour in the omelet batter and smooth the top with a spatula. Scatter the cooked bell pepper over the surface and reduce the heat to low.

Cover the skillet and cook for about 3 minutes, checking every 30 seconds to see if it's ready to fold. When the edges have dried, lift a section to see if the omelet is set. It should be golden, but not brown. Loosen the omelet by sliding the spatula underneath it, then fold the omelet in half. Cook for another minute, then slide the omelet onto a warm plate.

YIELD: 1 OMELET

The Hotta Frittata with Chopped Jalapeños

While the nutritional yeast gives this tofu-based frittata a welcome tangy edge and the dark rum provides the star power, a crash course in jalapeños is in order: These hot little numbers are a total tease, because they vary widely in heat content. Generally, if the outer skin of the pepper has lots of white streaks, called striations, the pepper will have ripened longer on the plant and will probably contain more capsaicin, which causes the heat to gather in the inner white ribs that surround the seeds. So if you want heat, select a pepper that has plenty of striations on the skin instead of a firm smooth pepper. And, if you *really* want to bring on the hot flash, use a habanero or Scotch bonnet pepper in addition to a jalapeño.

4 tablespoons extra-virgin olive oil

5 scallions, white and light green parts only, minced

2 cloves garlic, pressed

1 to 2 jalapeños, stemmed and minced

2 medium Yukon Gold potatoes, peeled and thinly sliced

1 teaspoon salt

Freshly ground black pepper to taste

12 ounces firm tofu, cubed and pressed to remove excess water (see instructions on page 31)

¼ cup low-sodium soy sauce

2 tablespoons dark rum

4 tablespoons nutritional yeast

Grated vegan cheese of choice (optional)

Preheat the oven to 325°F. In a large skillet, heat 2 tablespoons of the olive oil and sauté the scallions, garlic, and jalapeños for 3 minutes. Add the potatoes, salt, and pepper and cook for 12 minutes, stirring occasionally, until the potatoes begin to brown. Remove from the heat and let the mixture cool for a bit.

Pour the remaining 2 tablespoons of olive oil into a pie pan and spread it all around. In a food processor, combine the tofu, soy sauce, rum, and yeast and pulse until well mixed. Combine with the potato mixture and pour into the prepared pie pan. Roast for 45 minutes, until the top is firm and an inserted toothpick comes out clean. Sprinkle the top with the optional cheese and serve hot.

YIELD: 2 TO 4 SERVINGS

Très Chic French Toast

Bananas are used instead of eggs to give this fashionable brunch *classique* enough substance and sweetness to circumvent the need for maple syrup. However, if you dearly love syrup, go right ahead and use it—far be it from me to ever say no to self-indulgence! Meanwhile, the hallelujah of cognac added here lends the dish a silky, smooth touch that will insure it easily slides down the hatch.

2 to 3 ripe bananas, roughly sliced

¾ cup soy milk or other nondairy milk

1 tablespoon cognac

1 teaspoon cinnamon

1 teaspoon pumpkin pie spice

1 teaspoon vanilla extract

Potato bread, cut into 6 half-inch slices

Vegan margarine or canola oil

In a blender, combine the bananas, soy milk, cognac, cinnamon, pumpkin pie spice, and vanilla. Blend until smooth. Pour the mixture into a pie plate. Dip the bread slices in the mixture, coating both sides. Set aside briefly.

In a large skillet, melt the margarine over medium-high heat. Fry the bread slices until golden brown. Serve hot with maple syrup if desired.

YIELD: 6 SLICES OF FRENCH TOAST

Thrill on Blueberry-Coconut Hill Muffins

Even though these little gems look too pretty to eat, their mild rummy kick will ensure they disappear as quickly as you can pop them out of the oven and into your guests' mouths.

2 cups all-purpose flour

⅓ cup sugar

2 teaspoons baking powder

¼ teaspoon salt

½ cup soy milk or other nondairy milk

½ cup unsweetened coconut milk

2 tablespoons white rum

¼ cup vegan margarine, melted

Enough egg substitute to equal 1 egg

1 teaspoon lemon juice

1 cup fresh or thawed frozen blueberries

Preheat the oven to 400°F. In a large bowl, combine the flour, sugar, baking powder, and salt. Stir in the soy milk, coconut milk, rum, margarine, egg substitute, and lemon juice. Mix well. Gently stir in the blueberries.

Spoon the batter into a nonstick muffin pan (or grease the cups of a regular muffin pan), filling each cup about ⅔ full. Bake for 20 to 25 minutes, until the muffins are golden brown.

YIELD: 12 MUFFINS

Slur-Baaaaked Peaches with Cointreau

Peaches, brown sugar, and Cointreau join forces to give your *bruuuunch* feast a star-studded finale fit for the party monsters in your life, all with ease and laid-back elegance.

3 tablespoons chilled vegan margarine, cut into small cubes,
plus additional for greasing the baking dish

⅓ cup canned peach or apricot nectar

6 fresh peaches, peeled, halved, and pitted

2 tablespoons dark brown sugar

⅓ cup Cointreau, plus additional for serving

Vegan vanilla ice cream (See homemade Vanilla, I Scream!, page 148)

Preheat the oven to 375°F. Generously grease an 8 × 9-inch square baking dish with margarine. Pour the peach nectar into the dish and arrange the peach halves, cut side up, in the dish. Sprinkle with the brown sugar, drizzle with the Cointreau, and top with the 3 tablespoons of margarine cubes. Bake until the peaches are tender, about 30 minutes. Let the peaches cool for 10 minutes.

Scoop the vegan ice cream into six serving bowls, and spoon the two peach halves over each scoop. Divide the juices over all, and serve at once.

YIELD: 6 SERVINGS

THE LUSH'S LUNCH

"What contemptible scoundrel has stolen the cork to my lunch?"
—W. C. FIELDS

HERE'S SOMETHING
TO GET YOU STARTED ...

Hoochie-Coochie Margarita

This versatile seductress aims to please: if time is on your side, say a good 24 hours, the longer the zest and juice mixture steeps, the better. But if you're in a hurry (to get the good times rolling!), just omit the zest, skip the steeping process, and *get to it!*

4 teaspoons grated zest plus ½ cup juice from 3 medium limes

4 teaspoons grated zest plus ½ cup juice from 3 medium lemons

¼ cup white grapefruit juice

¼ cup superfine sugar

Pinch of salt, plus additional salt for rimming the glasses (optional)

2 cups crushed ice

1 cup tequila

1 cup triple sec

In a 1-quart glass measure, combine the lime zest and juice, lemon zest and juice, grapefruit juice, sugar, and salt. Cover with plastic wrap and refrigerate to let the flavors meld, at least 4 hours and up to 24 hours.

Divide 1 cup crushed ice among four to six Margarita glasses. Strain the juice mixture into a 1-quart pitcher. Add the tequila, triple sec, and the remaining crushed ice. Stir for 1 minute, or until thoroughly combined and chilled. Strain into ice-filled glasses and serve promptly.

YIELD: 1 QUART, SERVING 4 TO 6

STARTERS, SIDES, OR LIGHT MAIN DISHES

With a little help from your old pals—brandy, Madeira, cognac, vermouth, white wine, and beer—first impressions will be a breeze. This opening act of versatile dishes will captivate your fellow lunch lushes from the very beginning.

Chickpea, Roasted Pepper + Rosemary Rave on Zucchini Disks

For all those close encounters of the tasty kind, impress your guests from the start with these flavorful zucchini disks topped with homemade hummus and accented with brandy, or make them the stunning showstopper at your next happy hour or backyard rave.

2 (15-ounce) cans chickpeas, drained

1 small (6-ounce) jar roasted red peppers, drained well and coarsely chopped

½ lime, juiced

2 cloves garlic, pressed

4 stems fresh rosemary, leaves stripped from stems

Coarse salt and freshly ground black pepper

2 tablespoons extra-virgin olive oil, eyeball it as you drizzle it into recipe

2 tablespoons brandy

1 zucchini, sliced into ¼-inch disks

In a food processor, combine the chickpeas, red pepper, lime juice, garlic, rosemary, salt, and pepper. Turn the processor on and stream in the olive oil and the brandy. Spread the puree on zucchini disks and serve as an appetizer or side dish.

YIELD: 4 SERVINGS

Corn + Zucchini Sipping Sauté

Fresh from the local farmers' market or your own backyard garden (and the wine store!), this sipping sauté is high summer in a bowl. Cue the umbrella table flanked by hungry friends and plenty of cocktails to go around.

2 tablespoons extra-virgin olive oil

½ cup chopped scallions

1 clove garlic, pressed

2 cups corn, from about 4 ears

2 medium zucchini (1 pound total), quartered lengthwise, then cut into ¼-inch pieces

¼ teaspoon ground cumin

¼ teaspoon ground coriander

¼ teaspoon salt

⅛ teaspoon freshly ground black pepper

¼ cup Madeira

½ cup chopped fresh cilantro

In a 12-inch skillet, heat the oil over moderate heat until hot but not smoking, then cook the scallions, stirring constantly, until softened, about 3 minutes. Add the garlic and stir for 1 minute. Add the corn, zucchini, cumin, coriander, salt, pepper, and Madeira and cook, stirring occasionally, until the zucchini is tender, 4 to 6 minutes. Remove from the heat, stir in the cilantro, and season with salt and pepper. Serve in warmed bowls.

YIELD: 4 SERVINGS

Lentils in the Fast Lane

This feisty legume goes from zero to FUN in the blink of an eye with pearl onions, carrots, garlic, thyme, and a surprise appearance by vermouth.

10 ounces frozen pearl onions

2 tablespoons vegan margarine, or extra-virgin olive oil

1 large peeled carrot, cut diagonally into ⅛-inch thick slices

2 cloves garlic, pressed

1 teaspoon salt

½ teaspoon freshly ground black pepper

2 fresh thyme sprigs, or a pinch of dried thyme

1 bay leaf

1 cup dried French green lentils

2 cups water

½ cup dry vermouth or dry white wine

In a medium saucepan of water, boil the pearl onions for 1 minute, then drain.

Wipe out the saucepan and place it over moderate heat. Melt the margarine until the foam subsides, then cook the onions, carrots, garlic, salt, pepper, thyme, and bay leaf, stirring occasionally, until the vegetables are softened, 6 to 8 minutes.

Add the lentils, water, and vermouth and bring the mixture to a boil, then reduce heat and simmer, partially covered, until the lentils are just tender, 12 to 20 minutes. Discard thyme sprigs (if using) and bay leaf. Transfer lentils to a serving dish with a slotted spoon.

YIELD: 4 SERVINGS

NOTE: The cooking time of lentils varies pretty widely—the fresher they are, the faster they cook.

Lemony Lush Marinated Shiitake Mushrooms with Roasted Red Pepper

This is a sophisticated way to serve shiitake mushrooms, marinated in white wine and cognac, to your favorite lunch lushes, whether for business or an afternoon of pleasure.

1 pound, 2-inch shiitake mushroom caps

1 large sweet red pepper

MARINADE:

½ cup water

⅔ cup dry white wine (the better, the better)

1 teaspoon cognac

Juice of 1 large lemon

3 tablespoons extra-virgin olive oil

1 tablespoon porcini and/or garlic-infused extra-virgin olive oil

3 large shallots, minced

2 cloves garlic, minced

2 teaspoons fresh thyme leaves, or 1 teaspoon dry thyme

½ teaspoon dry oregano

½ teaspoon sea salt

9 crushed peppercorns

Freshly chopped chives and optional white truffle oil to garnish

Quarter the mushroom caps and set aside. Turn the pepper over a gas flame or under a broiler until black and sizzly, then sweat it in a closed paper bag. When cooled, rub off the blackened skin with paper towels and stem, seed, and cut the pepper into ¼-inch strips.

In a nonreactive saucepan, boil the marinade ingredients, covered loosely, for 10 minutes over medium-low heat. Strain thoroughly and return to pan. Add the mushrooms and bring back to a boil. Simmer very gently, uncovered, for 10 minutes, stirring occasionally.

Pour into a large glass bowl, fold in the pepper strips, and let marinate for 3 hours or so. Refrigerate, if you like (I prefer this at room temperature), but these should be consumed within 4 hours of preparation, lest the marinade overpower the mushrooms.

Before serving, finish with a dappling of chives and a light sprinkling of white truffle oil.

YIELD: 4 TO 6 SERVINGS

Corny Cele*brew*tante Salad

A little light beer adds a heavy touch of *awesome* to this colorful, farm-fresh salad that's fit for everyone from the Tinsel Town crowd to your favorite dive bar buddies.

6 large ears corn, shucked

1 tablespoon canola oil

1 jalapeño, stemmed, seeded, minced

Salt

1 clove garlic, pressed

1½ cups cooked or canned black beans, rinsed, drained, and at room temperature

2 ripe medium tomatoes, cored and diced

2 to 3 tablespoons light beer of choice

Fresh lime juice, to taste

Fresh chopped cilantro, for garnish

Stand an ear of corn in a shallow bowl, stem-side down. With a knife, slice the kernels off from top to bottom until all are removed. Continue with every ear.

Put a large cast-iron skillet over high heat and add oil. After 1 minute, add the corn and jalapeño. As the corn cooks, shake the pan to distribute it so that each kernel is deeply browned on at least one side.

Remove the skillet from the heat, then add salt to taste. Stir in the garlic and let it sit for 1 minute. Combine in a large bowl with the remaining ingredients. Taste, adjust seasoning, and serve. Serving options also include rolling the salad up in a whole wheat flour tortilla with chopped carrots and celery or serving it as a dip with tortilla chips.

YIELD: 4 SERVINGS

MAIN DISHES

When the curtain rises on these headlining dishes—starring vodka, Marsala, sherry, and beer—your guests will no doubt give your performance as the lunch host or hostess with the tipsy mostest *rave* reviews.

Three Tomatoes to the Wind Flan

It's high time for this tartlike bauble to have a triumphant comeback, Tipsy Vegan–style. For this swanky sparkler, tomato sauce and vodka are called upon to ensure that the fabulous flan is here to stay for a long, long time.

4 cloves garlic, peeled

2 (8-ounce) cans tomato sauce (Muir Glen or Del Monte)

¼ cup vodka

24 large basil leaves

½ cup extra-virgin olive oil

8 teaspoons unflavored vegan kosher gelatin, such as Lieber's Unflavored Jel

Salt and freshly ground black pepper to taste

24 slices country bread, 2 for each plate

In a food processor, mince the garlic cloves. Add the tomato sauce, vodka, twelve of the basil leaves, the olive oil, vegan gelatin, and salt and pepper to taste. Blend at high speed for 2 minutes.

Lightly oil twelve small cups or ramekins. Divide the tomato mixture among the cups and refrigerate for 20 minutes.

To serve, dip the bottom of each cup in hot water to loosen the flan. Unmold onto a plate. Garnish with a basil leaf and droplets of olive oil. Place two slices of bread on each plate.

YIELD: 12 SERVINGS

NOTE: If you can't find Lieber's Unflavored Jel (vegan gelatin), it's available online at VeganEssentials.com.

THE LUSH'S LUNCH

Staggering Eggplant Stacks

Calling all eggplants, it's time to pile on the fun! The best part: By the time you hit the bottom of this stack of Marsala-fueled bliss, you'll be feeling no pain.

1 (1 to 1¼-pound) purple or white eggplant, peeled

2 teaspoons kosher salt

4 tablespoons sun-dried tomato pesto of choice or the Sun-Dried Tomato Pesto on page 132

2 tablespoons nutritional yeast

¼ cup Marsala

Cut the eggplant crosswise into twelve ⅓-inch slices, discarding ends, and arrange in one layer on paper towels. Sprinkle both sides evenly with the salt and cover with another layer of paper towels. Let stand 30 minutes. Pat eggplant dry.

Preheat oven to 375°F and oil a shallow baking pan.

Arrange four eggplant slices in one layer in the pan and spread each slice evenly with 1 teaspoon of the pesto. Sprinkle 1 tablespoon of the nutritional yeast over the pesto on each slice. Continue to layer remaining eggplant slices, pesto, and yeast in the same manner. Bake in the middle of the oven until the eggplant is tender, 20 to 25 minutes. Serve dribbled with a little of the Marsala.

YIELD: 2 MAIN COURSE SERVINGS OR 4 SIDE DISHES

NOTE: White eggplants are firmer and less bitter than common purple eggplants, yet the skin is tougher and must be peeled.

THE LUSH'S LUNCH

Cozy Tofu Under Black Bean Sauce

Golden, crisp slices of tofu cozily arranged under a rich, warm blanket of black bean sauce mixed with a few swigs of sherry is now your main excuse for staying tucked inside on chilly afternoons.

1-pound block of extra-firm tofu, cut crosswise into 6 slices and pressed to remove excess water (see instructions on page 31)

4 cloves garlic

1-inch chunk of fresh ginger

2 tablespoons Chinese fermented black beans

1½ cups water

4 tablespoons soy sauce

3 tablespoons dry sherry

1 tablespoon maple syrup

2 teaspoons cider vinegar

1½ tablespoons cornstarch

Canola oil for frying

Prep the seasonings for the sauce: peel the garlic cloves and the ginger, then quarter the ginger. In a food processor, mince the garlic and ginger. In a small sieve, rinse the black beans until the water runs clear. Add them to the food processor and pulse until coarsely chopped.

In a medium bowl, stir together the water, soy sauce, sherry, maple syrup, vinegar, and cornstarch until the cornstarch is evenly suspended.

Generously film the bottom of a heavy 2-quart saucepan with the canola oil and heat over moderately high heat until hot but not smoking. Stir-fry the black bean mixture until fragrant, less than 1 minute. Stir the cornstarch mixture and add it to the pan. Whisk the sauce occasionally while bringing it to a boil and simmer for 1 minute. Set aside.

Generously film the bottom of a 12-inch nonstick skillet with the canola oil and heat over high heat until hot but not smoking. Blot up any excess moisture on the tofu with a paper towel before placing it in the skillet. Fry the slices on both sides, turning them only when the undersides are golden and crisp, 5 to 8 minutes total.

Reheat the sauce and serve the tofu, pouring the sauce over it. This pairs extremely well with rice and broccoli, or any other steamed vegetable of your choice.

YIELD: 3 TO 4 SERVINGS

Drunk Hummus in a Blanket

Classic seasonings, sweet onion, and basil combined with the tingly notes of red pepper and the golden rock star known as beer are all rolled into one pretty little package to keep your palate dancing all the way through lunch hour, or anytime. For parties, prepare several of these wraps and cut them into bite-size pieces to serve as hors d'oeuvres.

3 to 4 tablespoons red pepper hummus
(store-bought brand or homemade)

2 to 3 tablespoons beer (of choice)

Extra-virgin olive oil

1 slice flatbread (plain or flavor of choice) or
whole wheat flour tortilla shell

Garlic powder (to taste)

Italian seasoning (any kind)

1 fresh tomato, sliced

1 sweet onion, sliced (to taste)

Fresh basil

RED PEPPER HUMMUS:

1 red pepper, roasted until blackened, steamed in a
plastic bag, then skin rubbed off with paper towels,
stemmed and seeded, then roughly chopped

1 clove garlic, chopped

1 (14-ounce) can chickpeas, drained

½ cup tahini

⅓ cup freshly squeezed lemon juice

Kosher salt and freshly ground white pepper to taste

To prepare the hummus, in a food processor, combine the roasted red pepper, garlic, chickpeas, tahini, and lemon juice. Pulse until smooth, then season with the salt and white pepper.

Preheat oven to 375°F. In a bowl, combine the hummus and beer. Lightly brush the olive oil on the flatbread. Thinly spread the beer hummus mixture on the flatbread. Over the hummus, sprinkle the garlic powder and Italian seasoning. Place the tomatoes and onions over the mixture. Sprinkle everything again with Italian seasoning and olive oil. Top the mixture with the fresh basil. On foil, bake at 375 to 400°F for about 8 to 10 minutes, or until the tortilla is golden brown. Roll and serve as a wrap or open-faced.

YIELD: 1 SERVING

SWEET TREATS

The secret to an unforgettable finale for the ultimate lush's lunch is on the next page. Of course, no one will blame you if you and your guests head straight here first. Besides, who ever said dessert has to come last? Especially if time is of the essence and you *really* need that Noontime Quickie.

Apple Tree Compote

A soothing stand-alone dessert, this compote created with apple brandy also goes well with all kinds of savory entrées, such as when dribbled sparingly onto bowls of The Chugging Pumpkin Soup (page 36), served on the side with Wild Rice Under the Influence (page 53), or on top of your favorite coconut waffles. Of course, it also pulls double-duty as a satisfying midnight snack or a midday treat under the shade of your favorite old apple tree.

> 4 tablespoons (½ stick) vegan margarine, or ¼ cup applesauce
>
> 3 tart green apples, such as Granny Smith, peeled, cored, and chopped into ½-inch pieces
>
> 5 grates of whole nutmeg, or about ⅛ teaspoon ground nutmeg
>
> Pinch of ground allspice
>
> Pinch of ground cinnamon
>
> 5 to 6 grates of fresh, peeled ginger
>
> ¼ cup Calvados brandy (apple brandy) or apple liqueur

In a heavy skillet over low heat, melt the margarine or applesauce, and stir in the chopped apples, spices, and Calvados. Cover partially and simmer for 15 to 20 minutes. When just tender, move the apples to a glass bowl and keep warm.

YIELD: ABOUT 3 CUPS OF COMPOTE

NOTE: If using applesauce instead of margarine, be sure to stir the mixture more or less constantly until ready to serve.

Noontime Quickie

Want a noontime quickie? (Who doesn't every now and then!) This juiced, vodka smoothie will really get your afternoon off . . . to an energetic start.

> 1 ripe banana, sliced
>
> 1 cup orange juice, preferably freshly squeezed
>
> 1 cup soy milk or other nondairy milk
>
> 1 cup crushed ice
>
> ¾ cup vodka

In a blender, combine the ingredients and blend until smooth and thick.

YIELD: 1 SMOOTHIE

SLOSHED SUPPERS

"I like to drink martinis. Two at the most. Three I'm under the table, four I'm under the host."

—DOROTHY PARKER

HERE'S SOMETHING TO GET YOU STARTED ...

Extra! Extra! Dirty-Hot Martini

BREAKING NEWS: This firewater takes one of my all-time favorite thirst quenchers, the ever-popular dirty martini, in an even dirtier (*Oh my!*) and spicier (*Oh yes!*) new direction. Use the revved-up brine from a bottle of pickled jalapeños instead of olive juice to really show your guests you mean business when it comes to having fun.

However, if you still prefer to get down and dirty with olive juice, don't let me stop you. In fact, call and I'll be right over!

1½ ounces vodka or gin

1 teaspoon jalapeño pickling brine, or to taste

Sliced fresh or pickled jalapeño, to taste, or jalapeño-stuffed olives

In a cocktail shaker, combine the vodka or gin with the jalapeño pickling fluid and plenty of ice. Shake gently. Strain into a chilled martini glass and garnish with the jalapeño slices or jalapeño-stuffed olives.

YIELD: 1 MARTINI

The Boozer's Smoky + Spicy Baked Beans

Whether for a good ole backyard barbecue or a holiday feast, these buzzed beans will supercharge any occasion. The dark beer couples with the bourbon to give the beans deep background flavors and your guests an edible affair to remember.

2 tablespoons peanut oil

1 medium yellow onion, well chopped

¾ cup of your favorite barbecue sauce

¾ cup good dark beer of choice

¾ cup bourbon

3 tablespoons light molasses

2 tablespoons smooth Dijon mustard

1 tablespoon soy sauce

2 teaspoons 5-spice powder

4 teaspoons minced chipotle chiles canned with adobo sauce, and 1 to 2 teaspoons of the adobo sauce

1 (16-ounce) can Great Northern beans, drained

1 (16-ounce) can kidney beans, drained

1 (16-ounce) can black beans, drained

Preheat the oven to 350°F. In a large pot, heat the peanut oil over medium heat. When the oil slides easily across the pan, add the onion and sauté for 5 minutes, stirring often. Add the barbecue sauce, dark beer, bourbon, molasses, mustard, soy sauce, 5-spice powder, chipotles, and adobo sauce. Stir well, then add all the beans.

Transfer the bean mixture to a large gratin and bake, uncovered, until the liquid bubbles and thickens slightly, about 1 hour. Cool for 10 to 15 minutes before serving.

YIELD: 4 TO 6 SERVINGS

Baked + Loaded Acorn Squash

Sweeten your winter suppers with this loaded squash that can't help but warm you up from stem to stern when partnered with pears, Granny Smiths, nutmeg, cinnamon, and apple brandy.

4 acorn squash, halved, seeds and strings scooped out

3 tablespoons vegan margarine or extra-virgin olive oil

8 pears, peeled, cored, and diced

8 Granny Smith apples, peeled, cored, and diced

¼ cup Calvados brandy (apple brandy) or apple liqueur

Juice of 1 lemon

1½ teaspoons nutmeg

4 teaspoons cinnamon

Preheat the oven to 400°F. Place the halved squash on a sheet pan, skin side down. If necessary, cut a slice from the rounded side to make the squash level. Place 1 teaspoon (or so) of the margarine in each half, cover with foil, and bake until squash has softened, about 45 minutes. Remove from the oven.

Meanwhile, combine the diced pears and apples, and drizzle with the Calvados and lemon juice to prevent browning. Add nutmeg and cinnamon and stir until well mixed.

Spoon the mixture into squash halves, dividing evenly. Cover with foil and return to the oven. Bake until fruit is warmed through, about 15 minutes. Uncover and bake watchfully until slightly browned, about 5 minutes.

YIELD: 8 SERVINGS

Hot Toddy Tofu with Shiitakes

For those nonbelievers out there who still think that (*gasp!*) tofu is boring and tasteless, get ready to eat your words. Shiitakes, scallions, vegetable broth, soy sauce, and your choice of mirin or sherry revolutionize bean curd into an irresistibly tasty temptress.

1 pound extra-firm tofu, drained and sliced crosswise into ¾-inch thick slabs

2 tablespoons canola oil

1½ cups (4-ounces) thinly sliced shiitake mushroom caps

2 scallions, thinly sliced, dark green parts minced and reserved for garnish

¼ cup vegetable stock

1 teaspoon low-sodium soy sauce

2 teaspoons mirin (rice wine) or dry sherry

Pat the tofu dry with paper towels. In a large nonstick wok, heat the oil over medium-high heat. Place the tofu slabs in the wok and cook without disturbing, until golden on the bottom, 4 to 5 minutes. Turn and cook the other side 3 to 5 minutes longer. Dry the slabs on paper towels and keep them warm.

Increase the heat to high. Add the mushrooms and white and light green parts of the scallions. Cook, tossing occasionally, until the mushrooms are softened and light golden, about 3 minutes. Stir in the stock, soy sauce, and mirin. Cook until the sauce reduces and thickens slightly, about 1 minute longer.

Transfer the tofu to serving plates and top with the mushroom mixture and pan sauce. Sprinkle with the minced dark green scallions.

YIELD: 2 SERVINGS

Bottom's Up VegeBean Stew

Served warm on a snowy Sunday or chilled on a hot summer afternoon, a good basic golden lager or dark beer of choice tops off this festival of vegetables and beans, infusing the ingredients with the hearty twist and twang of earthy hops. Also, feel free to roll out a barrel of your own homebrew or favorite fresh ingredients, making this dish a true original every time.

1 (14½-ounce) can cut green beans

1 (15-ounce) can black beans

1 (15¼-ounce) can corn

1 (15-ounce) can light red kidney beans

1 (15½-ounce) can pinto beans

1 (15-ounce) can green and white lima beans

1 (14½-ounce) can green and shelled beans

1 quart (14-ounces) regular V-8 juice

1 (7-ounce) can peeled and chopped green chiles

2 (16-ounce) bags frozen stir-fry vegetables (thawed)

1 small head cabbage, chopped

¼ to ½ cup chopped fresh chives

2 to 4 (or to taste) tablespoons barley

3 tablespoons (or to taste) minced garlic

Season salt (to taste)

Garlic salt (to taste)

1 (12-ounce) bottle lager or dark beer (preferred) of choice

In a large pot, combine all the ingredients, except the beer. Cook, covered, over medium heat for 2½ to 3 hours, until the vegetables are soft. Slowly pour the beer into the pot about 45 minutes before serving. Simmer until ready to serve.

This is a very versatile dish. Feel free to experiment by adding other beans, vegetables, or seasonings (i.e., crushed red pepper flakes, vegan Worcestershire sauce, hot sauce) of choice. There is even a variety of V-8 juices, including a "Spicy Hot" version, that could each add a really unique kick to the stew.

YIELD: 12 TO 15 SERVINGS (I LIKE TO MAKE THIS MUCH JUST FOR ME ALONE AND THEN FREEZE THE REST IN SMALL CONTAINERS OF ONE TO TWO SERVINGS, FOR FUTURE MEALS OR TO GIVE TO FRIENDS AND NEIGHBORS.)

SLOSHED SUPPERS

Spicy Sesame Noodles Tie One On with Chopped Peanuts + Basil

Take your dinner guests on a culinary jaunt to the Far East and tie one on with this inspired dish where rice wine has its way with other classic ingredients like peanut oil, ginger, soy sauce, and rice noodles.

1 tablespoon peanut oil

2 tablespoons minced peeled fresh ginger

2 cloves garlic, pressed

3 tablespoons toasted sesame oil

2 tablespoons soy sauce

2 tablespoons balsamic vinegar

2 tablespoons rice wine

1½ tablespoons sugar

1 tablespoon (or more) hot chile oil

1½ teaspoons salt

1 pound fresh Chinese rice noodles (about ⅛ inch in diameter)

12 scallions, white and pale green parts only, thinly sliced

½ cup coarsely chopped roasted peanuts

¼ cup thinly sliced fresh Thai basil leaves

Salt and pepper to taste

In a small skillet, heat the peanut oil over medium heat. Add the ginger and garlic and sauté for 1 minute. Transfer to a large bowl. Add the sesame oil, soy sauce, balsamic vinegar, rice wine, sugar, chile oil, and salt and whisk to blend.

Place the fresh noodles in a sieve over the sink. Separate the noodles with your fingers and shake to remove excess starch. Cook in a large pot of boiling salted water until just tender, stirring occasionally. Drain and rinse under cold water until cool. Drain thoroughly and transfer to the bowl with the sauce. Add the scallions and toss to coat the noodles. Let stand at room temperature until the noodles have absorbed the dressing, tossing occasionally, about 1 hour. Stir in the peanuts and basil and toss again. Season to taste with the salt and pepper. Serve at room temperature.

YIELD: 4 SERVINGS

NOTE: The cooking time for rice noodles varies widely, so test often after a few minutes.

Angel Hair Pasta Knocks a Few Back with Devilish Pine Nuts + Lemon

When unexpected guests come a-knockin', this dish will be your trusted wingman. It can be ready in under 45 minutes, leaving plenty of time before *and* after supper for a few rounds of your favorite drinking games and other . . . hi-jinx.

¼ pound angel hair pasta or capellini

¾ teaspoon minced garlic

5 tablespoons extra-virgin olive oil

2 tablespoons pine nuts, toasted just until golden

2 tablespoons fresh lemon juice

2 teaspoons freshly grated lemon zest

2 tablespoons brandy

Salt and freshly ground black pepper

½ cup fresh bread crumbs

In a small skillet, cook the garlic in 2 tablespoons of the olive oil over medium-low heat, stirring, for 3 minutes. Transfer the garlic mixture to a large bowl, wipe out the skillet, and set it aside. Add the toasted pine nuts to the bowl, crushing them lightly with the back of a fork, then add the lemon juice, zest, brandy, salt, and pepper to taste.

Preheat the oven to 350°F. Spread the bread crumbs onto a small baking sheet and toast them until lightly browned, about 7 minutes. In the skillet, heat the remaining 3 tablespoons of olive oil over medium heat, transfer the toasted crumbs to the saucepan, and stir to coat well.

Cook the pasta in salted boiling water until al dente and, reserving 2 tablespoons of the cooking water, drain well. Add pasta with the reserved cooking water to bowl and toss with lemon mixture until it is absorbed. Toss again with the oiled crumbs. Serve at once.

YIELD: 2 SERVINGS

SLOSHED SUPPERS

Screwy Fusilli with Broccoli

This coterie of long, corkscrew pasta, broccoli florets, leeks, golden raisins, and vermouth makes for a very playful main course bonanza you can really sink your teeth into no matter the occasion.

1 large bunch broccoli, trimmed and cut into small florets

¼ cup dry vermouth or Madeira

½ cup extra-virgin olive oil

3 to 4 leeks, white and tender green parts, trimmed, rinsed well, and minced

4 cloves garlic, pressed

1 good pinch saffron threads

8 sun-dried tomatoes, packed in oil, drained, and minced

½ cup golden raisins

⅓ cup pine nuts, toasted

1 pound dried eggless fusilli

4 ounces vegan Parmesan cheese, freshly grated, about 1 cup, or nutritional yeast (optional)

Salt and freshly ground black pepper to taste

In a large bowl, microwave the broccoli in the vermouth just until slightly undercooked, about 5 to 10 minutes, depending on your oven, stirring after 3 minutes.

In a large skillet, heat ¼ cup of the olive oil over medium-high heat. Add the leeks and sauté until quite soft, about 10 minutes. Add the garlic and sauté for 1 minute longer. Stir in the saffron, sun-dried tomatoes, raisins, and pine nuts. Cook over low heat to blend the flavors, 5 to 6 minutes. Stir in the reserved broccoli.

Meanwhile, cook the fusilli in salted boiling water until al dente. Just before draining, ladle ¾ cup of the pasta cooking water into the sauce. Drain the fusilli thoroughly.

Toss the hot pasta with the sauce, mixing in the remaining ¼ cup of olive oil and the vegan Parmesan cheese. Season to taste with the salt and pepper (watch the salt!). Serve at once.

YIELD: 3 TO 4 SERVINGS

SLOSHED SUPPERS

Penne alla Vodka Martini

I always thought Penne alla Vodka needed the buttery, slightly herbal lilt of vermouth, benefiting by the way it works in a nice, velvety martini. The result is this voluptuous dish. Thickening the soy milk with cornstarch makes for a rich and creamy sauce completely without dairy. As for the crushed plum tomatoes, try to find a brand that doesn't pack them in tomato puree—it can make the sauce too thick. If the order of ingredients on the can begins with tomato puree, keep looking. Muir Glen crushed tomatoes are very good, but if you can find *real* imported San Marzano tomatoes, lunge. And you can always "crush your own" right in the can with a trusty fork. It takes a certain vigilance to stir and reduce the sauce for the last 10 minutes over spittingly high heat, but it's worth it, believe me. But be warned, all you kitchen daredevils: a splatter screen is practically essential.

1 large onion, well chopped	3 tablespoons tomato paste
2 tablespoons extra-virgin olive oil	1 cup soy milk or other nondairy milk
1 teaspoon dried red pepper flakes	1 to 2 tablespoons cornstarch
1 (28-ounce can) crushed San Marzano plum tomatoes	1 pound good dried penne rigate
	Oregano, fresh chopped or dried
¾ cup vodka	More dried red pepper flakes, if desired
½ cup dry vermouth	

In a good, deep, heavy-duty sauté pan, cook the onion in the olive oil over moderate heat until soft and translucent, stirring often, about 5 minutes. Sprinkle the red pepper flakes over the onion, then add the crushed tomatoes, lower the heat, and simmer for 30 minutes, stirring every 5 to 10 minutes.

Meanwhile, bring a large pot of salted water to a boil for the penne, which will probably need no more than about 10 to 12 minutes to cook, so don't add it to the boiling water until the final phase.

Stir the vodka, vermouth, and tomato paste into the tomato mixture. Simmer for 15 minutes.

Meanwhile, thicken the soy milk by heating it in a glass measure in a microwave oven or over medium heat in a small saucepan. Just as it's about to boil, stir in 1 tablespoon of cornstarch. If the soy milk doesn't thicken, add the additional tablespoon of cornstarch.

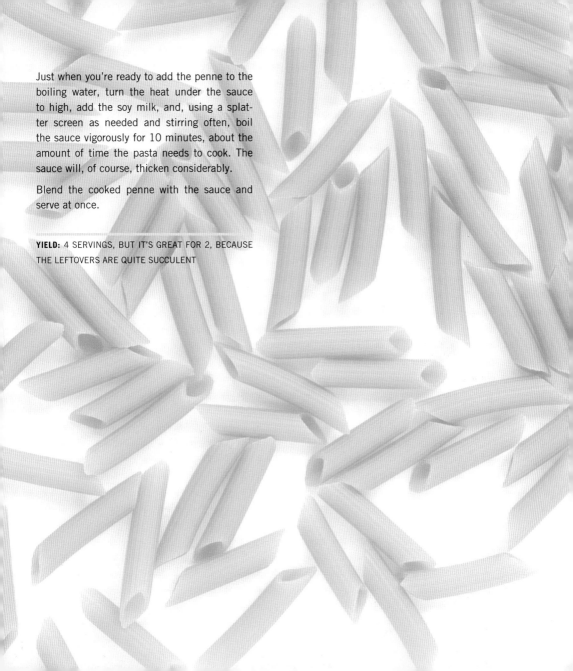

Just when you're ready to add the penne to the boiling water, turn the heat under the sauce to high, add the soy milk, and, using a splatter screen as needed and stirring often, boil the sauce vigorously for 10 minutes, about the amount of time the pasta needs to cook. The sauce will, of course, thicken considerably.

Blend the cooked penne with the sauce and serve at once.

YIELD: 4 SERVINGS, BUT IT'S GREAT FOR 2, BECAUSE THE LEFTOVERS ARE QUITE SUCCULENT

Towering Spaghetti Inferno

This inexpensive, leaning tower of pasta made with chipotle chiles, Marsala, tomato paste, and pine nuts comes together quickly for last-minute parties and celebrations, all to remind you and your guests what it really means to eat, laugh, and live *la dolce vita*.

1 pound spaghetti

2 tablespoons canola oil

1 medium yellow onion, diced

1 (7-ounce) can chipotle chiles in adobo sauce

½ cup Marsala (or dry vermouth)

2 tablespoons tomato paste or ketchup

2 tablespoons pine nuts, toasted

Lots of freshly grated vegan Parmesan cheese, or nutritional yeast (optional)

Bring a large pot of salted water to a rolling boil and cook the spaghetti until al dente, about 11 minutes.

In a large skillet, heat the oil over medium-high heat and sauté the onion, stirring frequently, until the onion is translucent.

Meanwhile, in a mini-processor, pulse the chipotles and their sauce with the Marsala and tomato paste until fairly smooth, but not completely pureed.

Deglaze the skillet by adding a little Marsala or water and scraping up any browned bits with a wooden spoon. Add the chipotle mixture and the pine nuts to the skillet, and reduce the heat to medium low. Cook the mixture until heated through, about 10 minutes.

Drain the spaghetti and toss with the sauce. Serve with plenty of vegan Parmesan cheese, if desired.

YIELD: 4 SERVINGS

Pizza Par-taaay with Sun-Dried Tomato Pesto

Mangia, mangia! It's time for you to host the best pizza par-*taaay* ever, with the help of your good friends, vodka and sherry.

PIZZA:

1 prebaked thin vegan pizza crust

¼ cup vodka

1 teaspoon finely chopped fresh rosemary leaves

½ teaspoon crushed dried red pepper flakes

1 teaspoon dried oregano

Toppings of choice (i.e., mushrooms, onions, peppers, sautéed spinach, nutritional yeast, etc.)

SUN-DRIED TOMATO PESTO:

¼ cup basil leaves, tightly packed

¼ cup toasted and salted almonds, roughly chopped

¼ cup toasted pine nuts

2 cloves garlic, peeled and chopped

½ teaspoon lemon zest

½ teaspoon lime zest

2 generous pinches kosher salt

2 grinds white pepper, or to taste

½ dozen small to medium dry sun-dried tomatoes (see note below), reconstituted in 1 cup dry sherry, or white wine, for 20 minutes or until softened, then drained (the reconstituted sun-dried tomatoes should equal about 1 cup)

2 tablespoons of the dry sherry or dry white wine, reserved, plus additional if needed

¾ cup extra-virgin olive oil

1 tablespoon balsamic vinegar

NOTE: If you can find them, use dry sun-dried tomatoes. They tend to be far less salty than those packed in oil. But if they're not available, use bottled and rinse them well. .

Preheat the oven to 450°F. Place the pizza crust on a baking sheet. Rub the crust with the vodka. Sprinkle evenly with the rosemary, red pepper flakes, and oregano.

To prepare the pesto: In a food processor, combine all the pesto ingredients and pulse until smooth, adding more sherry (or white wine) if needed (yields about 1½ to 2 cups).

Spread 1 cup of the pesto evenly over the crust, add your topppings of choice, and bake watchfully, 10 to 12 minutes, or according to directions given on the prebaked crust.

YIELD: 1 PIZZA

NOTE: For any leftover pesto, cover it with plastic wrap, pressing the plastic right onto the surface of the pesto. It can then be later used as a delicious spread on whole-grain toast, in a salad dressing, to make the Staggering Eggplant Stacks on page 111, or freeze it for a quick weeknight pizza supper.

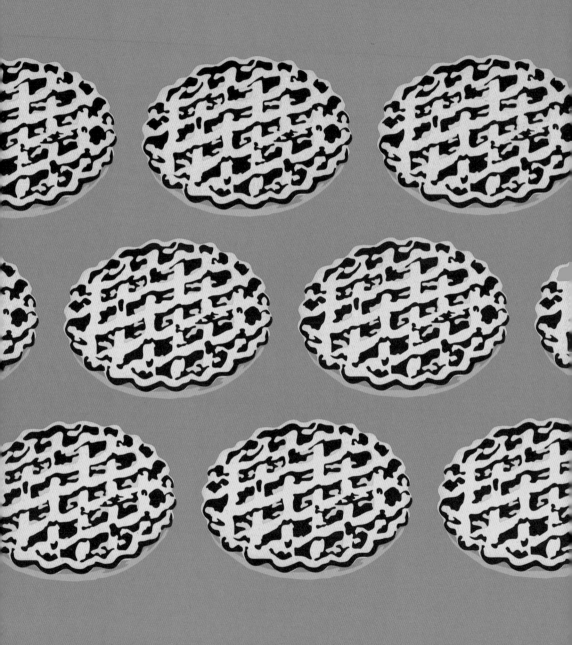

DRUNKEN DESSERTS

8

You're not drunk if you can lie on the floor without holding on."
—DEAN MARTIN

HERE'S SOMETHING
TO GET YOU STARTED ...

Zippy Mint Cocktail

Whether you're looking for the perfect after-dinner drink, or you prefer to drink your dessert, the minty freshness of this zippy cocktail will make you the coolest party *kat* on the block!

Several mint sprigs, for steeping and garnishing

12 ounces dry Chardonnay

8 ounces gin

2 ounces crème de menthe

In a large glass pitcher, soak the mint sprigs for 2 hours in half the Chardonnay. Add the remaining Chardonnay, the gin, and the crème de menthe. In a cocktail shaker, shake well with plenty of ice and strain into chilled martini glasses. Place a fresh mint sprig in each glass.

YIELD: 6 COCKTAILS

Bing-Bang-Boom Cherry Sauce

Behold, here's the ultimate cherry on top of any great feast. With its inspired dose of brandy, this dessert will deliver a BING-BANG-BOOM-BOOM-POW every time!

2 tablespoons vegan margarine

1 to 2 tablespoons sugar, depending on the sweetness
of the cherries

½ teaspoon salt

¼ cup water

1 pound Bing cherries, stemmed and pitted and halved,
reserving as much juice as possible, but not obsessively

⅓ cup brandy, Kirsch, Cointreau, or cognac

Freshly squeezed lemon juice, to taste (at least 1 tablespoon)

1 teaspoon lemon (or orange) zest

1 tablespoon cornstarch dissolved in 2 tablespoons water

Vegan vanilla ice cream (See homemade Vanilla, I Scream! page 148)

In a 1-quart saucepan, melt the margarine over medium heat. Add the sugar, salt, and water, stirring until the sugar and salt dissolve completely, then add all the cherries with any juices. Keep stirring until the mixture heats, about 6 minutes. Pour in the liquor, stir to blend well, bring to a boil, then simmer for 3 to 4 minutes. Stir in the lemon juice and zest, then taste carefully, adjusting the flavor with sugar or more lemon if necessary. Remember, this will be over ice cream, so you don't want it too sweet.

Pour in the cornstarch mixture and stir over medium-low heat until the sauce thickens. Spoon the warm sauce over a scoop or two of vegan ice cream.

YIELD: ABOUT 1 PINT OF SAUCE

DRUNKEN DESSERTS

You're the Boss, Applesauce!

One thing's for sure: This isn't the applesauce you remember from your grade school cafeteria. Just as variety is the spice of life, it turns out the same is true of applesauce, especially when it's rendered three sheets to the wind with apple brandy. And if you really want to make it go *POP!* use a mix of apples, such as Pippins, McIntosh, and Golden Delicious.

3 pounds apples (see headnote), cut into ½-inch slices

½ cup cider

1 tablespoon fresh lemon juice

1 cinnamon stick

½ cup sugar

1 teaspoon ground ginger

Several grates of nutmeg

¾ cup Calvados brandy (apple brandy) or apple liqueur

In a large kettle, mix the sliced apples with the cider and lemon juice, and drop in the cinnamon stick. Cover the pot and simmer, stirring often, over low heat, until the apples are tender, but not too mushy, about 20 minutes.

Stir in the remaining ingredients. Bring to a simmer, stirring to dissolve the sugar, about 1 minute. Remove and discard the cinnamon stick. Let the mixture cool, then pass it through a food mill. Serve warm or chilled.

YIELD: 4 TO 6 SERVINGS

NOTE: One of the advantages of using a food mill is that you don't have to bother coring or peeling the apples before cooking.

DRUNKEN DESSERTS

Buzzed Blueberry Pie with an Oatmeal Crust

This is ooey-gooey, utter fabulousness cradled in an oatmeal crust. The boozed-up berry-licious filling tastes especially fresh because of the presence of a whole tablespoon of orange zest—and, if you want, a bit of lemon zest. I don't add sugar to the filling, because I don't like fruit to be cloyingly sweet, but by all means suit yourself. Be forewarned: the first piece cut from the pie will usually be a flowing, delicious, hot mess that you'll want to jump right into.

CRUST:

2 cups rolled oats, or "old-fashioned" oatmeal

1 cup all-purpose flour

¾ cup dark brown sugar

½ teaspoon sea salt

1 teaspoon cinnamon

6 grates of nutmeg

1 teaspoon vanilla extract

12 tablespoons (1½ sticks) of vegan margarine, melted, plus extra for greasing the pie pan

FILLING:

4 cups fresh or thawed frozen blueberries, picked over, washed at the last minute, and dried gently with paper towels

1 heaping tablespoon orange zest, finely minced, or more, if you like

1 teaspoon lemon zest, finely minced (optional)

2 tablespoons all-purpose flour

2 tablespoons triple sec

Preheat oven to 325°F. Grease a 10-inch glass pie pan (for a thick crust; 12-inch for thin). In a food processor fitted with a steel blade, process the oats, flour, brown sugar, salt, cinnamon, nutmeg, and vanilla to blend. Add the melted margarine and process just until combined. The dough will be stiff. Press the dough into and up the sides of the prepared pan. Bake for 15 minutes.

Meanwhile, in a low, wide bowl, gently combine all the filling ingredients. Pour the mixture into the prebaked crust and return to the oven for 25 minutes, or just until the crust begins to brown lightly. Cool on a wire rack.

Serve warm or at room temperature with a scoop of Vanilla, I Scream! (page 148).

YIELD: 1 (10- OR 12-INCH) PIE

Hunky Granola Gets Hammered

While I'm not a mathematical genius by any stretch of the imagination, I'm digging the algebraic instructions for this earthy granola that is fit for hippie or hipster. If only all of life's equations were this easy and delicious (and full of triple sec!). But fear not, in the Tipsy Vegan world, everyone gets an A+.

(A)	(B)	(C)
6 cups rolled oats	½ cup peanut oil	1 cup plump raisins
1 cup coconut	½ cup sugar	½ cup dried blueberries, cranberries,
¾ cup wheat germ	⅓ cup water	or cherries (optional)
½ cup sunflower seeds	1 tablespoon vanilla	
1 teaspoon kosher salt	2 tablespoons maple syrup	
1 teaspoon cinnamon	¼ cup triple sec	

Combine (a) in a very large bowl. Mix (b) in a large bowl and pour over (a). Stir until all bits are coated. Spread on two large, parchment-lined jelly roll pans in one layer. Bake at 350°F for 21 minutes, stirring every 7 minutes. Remove from the oven if the mixture is getting too brown. Cool thoroughly and add (c). Store in a tightly covered container or two.

YIELD: ABOUT 2 QUARTS OF GRANOLA

Cockeyed Cranberry Compote

It's official, the Tipsy Vegan has spoken: You don't have to wait for the holidays to go all-out gluttonous with this crazy-cool cranberry extravaganza. The red berries and dry vermouth starring in this dish are up for the job anytime you want, including as a sweet side-dish accent, a spread for your favorite biscotti, or as a perky topper for a bowl of hot oatmeal. Now that deserves a round of *cheers!*

12 ounces (about 3 cups) cranberries

¾ cup dry vermouth (or slightly less), port, or dry red wine (the heavier, the better)

¼ cup balsamic vinegar

⅓ cup sugar (or to taste, as cranberries can vary in sourness)

2 pinches of kosher salt

Juice and zest of 1 orange

1 teaspoon fresh lemon juice

1 teaspoon lemon zest

1 teaspoon cornstarch

½ teaspoon dry mustard

Pinches of ground cloves, allspice, and ginger, or pumpkin pie seasoning

¼ cup golden raisins, reconstituted in hot water or hot fruity red wine (optional)

In a heavy large saucepan, combine the berries, dry vermouth, and balsamic vinegar over medium-high heat. Cook until most of the berries burst, stirring occasionally, about 10 minutes.

Add the sugar and salt, and stir for 1 minute.

Meanwhile, in a medium bowl, combine the orange juice and zest, lemon juice and zest, cornstarch, mustard, and spices; whisk until smooth. Stir into the hot berry mixture.

Stir in the optional raisins. Simmer until thickened, about 5 minutes.

Taste carefully for sweetness.

YIELD: ABOUT 2 CUPS

DRUNKEN DESSERTS

Bad-Ass Beer Cake with Bourbon Raisins + Amaretto Frosting

Beer. And bourbon. And amaretto! *Together in one cake!* **No, you're not dreaming. This is just how we roll in the Tipsy Vegan world. Commence indulging . . .**

1 cup golden raisins

Enough warm bourbon to immerse the raisins

5 cups all-purpose flour

½ teaspoon cinnamon

½ teaspoon mace

3 cups sugar

1¼ cups vegan margarine (2½ sticks)

Egg substitute to equal 3 eggs

1½ tablespoons baking powder

½ teaspoon salt

2 cups pale ale

Amaretto frosting (see directions below)
(or frosting of choice)

Preheat the oven to 350°F. In a large glass measure, place the raisins and pour in enough warmed bourbon to cover them. Let the raisins soak for 20 minutes.

To prepare the topping: in a medium bowl, mix 1 cup of the flour with the cinnamon, mace, and 1 cup of the sugar. Mix in ½ cup of the margarine (1 stick) and set aside.

In a standing mixer, beat the remaining sugar and margarine until well blended and creamy. Add the egg substitute and beat well.

Sift the remaining 4 cups of flour with the baking powder and salt and add them to the batter, 1 cup at a time. Finally, fold in the beer and the drained raisins.

Transfer the mixture to an oiled 10-inch cake pan. Evenly sprinkle on the topping.

Bake for 1 hour, or until an inserted toothpick comes out clean. Let the cake cool completely, then spread on the Amaretto Frosting.

AMARETTO FROSTING:

12 (1-ounce) squares semi-sweet vegan chocolate

¾ cup amaretto

1 cup (2 sticks) vegan margarine

Roughly chop the chocolate and place it in a medium saucepan. Pour the amaretto over the chocolate and turn the heat to low. Stir continually until the chocolate is almost completely melted. Remove from the heat and keep stirring until the mixture is smooth.

Cut the margarine into ½-inch pieces and beat it into the chocolate mixture with a fork, 1 piece at a time. Refrigerate the frosting until it reaches a spreadable consistency, about ½ hour. (Makes about 2 cups, or enough for one cake.)

YIELD: 1 (10-INCH) CAKE

NOTE: If you don't have a nearby source for vegan chocolate, it's available online at VeganEssentials.com.

Vanilla, I Scream!

Get ready to scream your head off for this vanilla utopia in a bowl. This is one smooth, sweet, vodka-infused dessert you'll indulge in time and again, *and again, and again*—whether by itself or when it's hooking up with the likes of Bing-Bang-Boom Cherry Sauce (page 137), Buzzed Blueberry Pie with an Oatmeal Crust (page 140), or Slur-Baaaaked Peaches with Cointreau (page 92).

½ cup cream of coconut milk

1 cup soy milk or other nondairy milk

½ cup sugar

8 ounces silken tofu, cubed and pressed to remove excess water (see instructions on page 31)

1 tablespoon vanilla extract

Seeds scraped from ½ vanilla bean (wrap and refrigerate the other ½ of the bean for another use)

2 to 3 tablespoons vanilla-flavored vodka

Place all the ingredients into a standing blender and blend until thoroughly pureed. Pour the mixture into an ice cream machine and freeze according to the manufacturer's instructions. Transfer to the freezer and freeze for at least 3 hours.

YIELD: ABOUT 3 CUPS

THE SPINNING
SORBET BAR

For your entertainment, the illustrious sorbet joins an esteemed ensemble cast of superstars from the bar circuit: tequila, Merlot, vodka, triple sec, and apple and peach brandy. With these little divas, it's always opening night in someone's mouth.

Merlot Ice Ice, Baby!

For a sophisticated palate cleanser or light after-dinner dessert, this frozen Merlot blend will satisfy even your most discerning guests, not to mention it will dazzle your favorite wine snobs.

3 cups water

⅔ cup sugar

1½ cups Merlot

½ teaspoon cinnamon (optional)

In a medium saucepan, combine the water and sugar. Bring to a boil, stirring occasionally. Remove from heat and let cool. Stir in the Merlot. Pour the mixture into an 8-inch square pan. Cover and freeze for 3 hours or until firm, stirring occasionally.

Break frozen mixture into chunks. Place the chunks in a food processor and pulse until smooth, scraping down the sides of the work bowl if necessary. Return slush mixture to the 8-inch pan, cover, and freeze for 3 hours or until firm.

YIELD: ABOUT 1 QUART

Barfly Banana Sorbet

Wait. For. It . . . Yep, it's bananas! B-A-N-A-N-A-S with V-O-D-K-A!

4 overripe medium bananas

½ cup cold water

¾ cup sugar (slightly less if the bananas are very sweet)

2 tablespoons fresh lemon juice

1 tablespoon vodka

In a food processor, puree the bananas with the water until the mixture is very smooth. Pour into a large metal bowl. Add the remaining ingredients and whisk to blend well. Cover the bowl and refrigerate for at least 3 hours.

Whisk the mixture again. Freeze it in an ice cream machine following the manufacturer's instructions. Transfer to a quart-size container, cover tightly, and freeze for at least 2 hours.

YIELD: ABOUT 1 QUART

NOTE: When bananas develop speckles, transfer them to the refrigerator for a few days. Even if the skins turn black, the bananas will work well in this recipe.

Margarita Sorbet Down the Hatch

Cool down with this icy scoop of tequila heaven while frolicking by the pool, the sea, or, *oh hell*, even the creek. Swimsuits optional, of course.

½ cup sugar

1 cup lime juice from about 8 limes, and the finely grated zest of the limes

3 cups freshly squeezed grapefruit juice

¼ teaspoon salt

½ cup tequila

In a small saucepan, stir the sugar into the lime juice. Bring to a boil and stir until the sugar is completely dissolved. Let the mixture cook for a few minutes, then stir in the grapefruit juice, salt, and tequila. Chill the mixture and then freeze in an ice cream machine according to the manufacturer's instructions.

YIELD: ABOUT 1 QUART

Bi-Curious Orange Sorbet

An enticing choice accompanies this rich crimson-hued sorbet: Orange liqueur or vodka? Of course, you could always satiate *everyone's* appetite and make both variations, giving all your guests the full monty.

3 pounds blood oranges (8 to 10 medium oranges), for 2 cups of juice

1 cup sugar

1 tablespoon fresh lemon juice

1 tablespoon orange liqueur (such as triple sec, Cointreau, or Grand Marnier) or vodka

Rinse and dry 1 or 2 of the oranges and grate 2 teaspoons of zest from their skins.

Squeeze 2 cups of juice from the oranges. Strain to remove any seeds.

In a large bowl, combine the orange zest, orange juice, sugar, lemon juice, and liqueur. Whisk to blend. Cover and refrigerate until very cold, at least 2 hours and as long as 3 days.

Whisk the mixture to blend and pour into the canister of an ice cream maker. Freeze according to the manufacturers instructions. Transfer to a covered container and freeze until firm, at least 1 hour or as long as 3 days.

YIELD: ABOUT 3 CUPS

Hocus-Pocus Cider + Pear Sorbet

This late autumn brandy sorbet is the perfect palate-pleaser for any guest, be they trick *or* treat.

1 pound Granny Smith apples, peeled, cored, and finely chopped

1 pound ripe Bartlett pears, peeled, cored, and finely chopped

1 cup apple cider

2 tablespoons Calvados (apple brandy) or apple liqueur

1 teaspoon almond extract

½ cup sugar, or more to taste

½ cup cold water

1 cinnamon stick

4 whole cloves

2 teaspoons roughly grated orange zest

½ cup fresh lemon juice

In a medium saucepan, combine the apples, pears, ½ cup of the cider, and 1 tablespoon of the Calvados over medium heat. Bring to a boil, then reduce the heat to low and simmer, stirring frequently, for 10 minutes, or until the apples have softened. Remove from the heat, stir in the remaining 1 tablespoon of Calvados and the almond extract and allow to cool. Puree the mixture thoroughly with an immersion blender. Cover and refrigerate until thoroughly chilled, at least 1 hour.

In a medium heavy saucepan, combine the sugar with the water, cinnamon stick, cloves, and orange zest. Bring the mixture to a boil, stirring, until the sugar is dissolved. Set aside to let the syrup steep for 10 minutes, then add the lemon juice and refrigerate until thoroughly chilled, at least 1 hour.

Strain the syrup through a fine sieve. Discard the cinnamon stick, cloves, and orange zest. Place 2½ cups of the apple-pear puree in a bowl. Stir in the syrup and the remaining ½ cup of cold cider and blend well with an immersion blender. Pour the mixture into an ice cream machine and freeze according to the manufacturer's instructions.

YIELD: ABOUT 1 QUART

DRUNKEN DESSERTS

Peachy Potion #17 Sorbet

And just what exactly does this mysterious Potion #17 do? Let's just say, with its smooth blend of peaches and brandy it reconfirms what you should already know by now: Tipsy Vegans *rule* when it comes to having fun! Now, party on . . .

1½ pounds ripe peaches (about 6 medium), peeled and pitted

½ cup cold filtered water

⅔ cup sugar, or to taste

2 tablespoons fresh lemon juice

1 tablespoon peach brandy

In a food processor or blender, puree the peaches with the water until smooth. Pour into a 1-quart container. Taste the puree for sweetness, then add the appropriate amount of sugar, lemon juice, and peach brandy to the peach puree. Stir to blend. Cover and refrigerate until very cold, at least 2 hours, or put the covered bowl in the freezer until very cold, about 1 hour.

Stir the mixture to blend it again, and pour into the canister of an ice cream maker. Freeze according to the manufacturer's directions. Return to the 1-quart measure and freeze until firm, at least 1 hour.

YIELD: ABOUT 1 QUART

Intense Pucker-Up Lemon Sorbet

The faint of heart need not apply: If you're not careful, this commanding sorbet with its lemon and vodka might just take a bite out of you first. *Meow!*

1 cup fresh lemon juice (from about 6 lemons)

Zest of 3 lemons

1 cup cold water

1 cup (or a bit less) of quick-dissolving ("superfine") sugar

1 tablespoon vodka

In a large, nonreactive bowl, blend together all the ingredients. Stir until the sugar dissolves completely. Refrigerate the mixture, covered, until thoroughly chilled, at least 45 minutes.

Churn the mixture in an ice cream machine according to the manufacturer's instructions until frozen, 20 to 30 minutes. Scoop the sorbet into a freezable container, and freeze it for at least 2 hours.

The sorbet keeps well for 3 to 4 days; then it usually hardens considerably.

YIELD: ABOUT ⅔ QUART

DRUNKEN DESSERTS

AFTERWORD (A.K.A. THE NIGHTCAP)

In addition to introducing me to martinis (for which no amount of gratitude could ever suffice), my Grandma Skok and Great Aunt Helen taught me two of life's most valuable lessons: One, laughter can be found in absolutely every situation. After all, life is ultimately meant to be a party. And, two, before parting ways with loved ones after a celebration, you should *always* have one last drink together.

With its velvety mint kick and soothing knack for rejuvenating the body, the classic Stinger was always one of Grandma's and Helen's favorite ways to add an exclamation point to a good time filled with friends, food, and laughter. And now, it's one of mine.

While the cliché tells us that "all good things must come to an end," we in the Tipsy Vegan world know better. Therefore, I hope this special cocktail is only the first of many last drinks, exclamation points, and laughs you and I will share together, my friend.

Until we meet again . . . Rock the Kitchen (and the Bar)!

The Laughing Stinger

One or two of these babies and you'll float like a butterfly. Three or more, and you'll not only sting like a bee, you'll be buzzing around like one, too. Chin-chin!

1 shot brandy

1 shot white crème de menthe

Fill a cocktail glass to the top with ice. Add the shots, and stir. Add more ice if necessary to fill the glass. Be sure to serve this cocktail very, very cold.

YIELD: 1 COCKTAIL

METRIC CONVERSIONS

- The recipes in this book have not been tested with metric measurements, so some variations might occur.
- Remember that the weight of dry ingredients varies according to the volume or density factor: 1 cup of flour weighs far less than 1 cup of sugar, and 1 tablespoon doesn't necessarily hold 3 teaspoons.

GENERAL FORMULA FOR METRIC CONVERSION

Ounces to grams	ounces $\times$ 28.35 = grams
Grams to ounces	grams $\times$ 0.035 = ounces
Pounds to grams	pounds $\times$ 453.5 = grams
Pounds to kilograms	pounds $\times$ 0.45 = kilograms
Cups to liters	cups $\times$ 0.24 = liters
Fahrenheit to Celsius	(°F − 32) $\times$ 5 ÷ 9 = °C
Celsius to Fahrenheit	(°C $\times$ 9) ÷ 5 + 32 = °F

VOLUME (LIQUID) MEASUREMENTS

1 teaspoon = ⅙ fluid ounce = 5 milliliters
1 tablespoon = ½ fluid ounce = 15 milliliters
2 tablespoons = 1 fluid ounce = 30 milliliters
¼ cup = 2 fluid ounces = 60 milliliters
⅓ cup = 2⅔ fluid ounces = 79 milliliters
½ cup = 4 fluid ounces = 118 milliliters
1 cup or ½ pint = 8 fluid ounces = 250 milliliters
2 cups or 1 pint = 16 fluid ounces = 500 milliliters
4 cups or 1 quart = 32 fluid ounces = 1,000 milliliters
1 gallon = 4 liters

VOLUME (DRY) MEASUREMENTS

¼ teaspoon = 1 milliliter
½ teaspoon = 2 milliliters
¾ teaspoon = 4 milliliters
1 teaspoon = 5 milliliters
1 tablespoon = 15 milliliters
¼ cup = 59 milliliters
⅓ cup = 79 milliliters
½ cup = 118 milliliters
⅔ cup = 158 milliliters
¾ cup = 177 milliliters
1 cup = 225 milliliters
4 cups or 1 quart = 1 liter
½ gallon = 2 liters
1 gallon = 4 liters

OVEN TEMPERATURE EQUIVALENTS, FAHRENHEIT (F) AND CELSIUS (C)

100°F = 38°C
200°F = 95°C
250°F = 120°C
300°F = 150°C
350°F = 180°C
400°F = 205°C
450°F = 230° C

WEIGHT (MASS) MEASUREMENTS

1 ounce = 30 grams
2 ounces = 55 grams
3 ounces = 85 grams
4 ounces = ¼ pound = 125 grams
8 ounces = ½ pound = 240 grams
12 ounces = ¾ pound = 375 grams
16 ounces = 1 pound = 454 grams

LINEAR MEASUREMENTS

½ in = 1½ cm
1 inch = 2½ cm
6 inches = 15 cm
8 inches = 20 cm
10 inches = 25 cm
12 inches = 30 cm
20 inches = 50 cm

ACKNOWLEDGMENTS

The road to this moment has been long and filled with many shining stars to whom I owe more thanks than I can ever adequately acknowledge. But here's my best shot:

To my parents, Jack and Barb, who first taught me compassion for *all* living beings, great and small, and what good cooking is.

To Jonathan Safran Foer, who through his groundbreaking work, *Eating Animals*, opened my eyes with a single word on page 266. And, Michelle Aielli, publicist-extraordinaire and cherished friend, who made the connection that sparked a personal revolution.

To Ellen DeGeneres and her amazing team at *The Ellen DeGeneres Show* (especially Kara and Dee), who gave me a voice and an opportunity to connect with millions of my neighbors across the country during an inspired moment that changed my world forever and planted the seeds of this book.

To my editor, Renee Sedliar, who understood the sheer FUN and potential of this project from the very first moment she heard about it. Likewise, I knew from the start that she would be one of the most creative and enthusiastic editors with whom I will ever have the honor of working.

To the brilliant team at Da Capo Lifelong, including associate director of editorial services Cisca Schreefel, copy editor Martha Whitt, proofreader Lori Lewis, indexer Jean DeBarbieri, and designer Megan Jones. Your dedication and talent for raising the bar (pun intended) when it comes to creating the best books, including this one (if I do say so myself), have rocked the planet time and again.

To Tom Steele, who generously shared his culinary genius with me, helping to make this book as flavorful and spicy as it could be.

To Amy Beadle Roth, whose breathtaking photography makes the food look like you could eat it right off the page. You're one of the very best.

To Steve Troha, who is the absolute best and most visionary agent anyone could ever hope for—thanks most of all for sharing my vision that life is meant to be a party!

And, finally, to Little Coyote, who sleeps soundly under my desk everyday as I write. Discovered alone—frightened, bald, and nearly starved beneath an old abandoned car, he held on and found his way into my home and my heart because he knew there was a place in this world where he would be loved. He is my muse and my co-author in more ways than I can ever explain.

In other words . . . to all the above and to every two-legged, four-legged, winged, finned, buzzing, and even slithering being whom I meet in my adventures, I will forever be grateful that our paths crossed in this lifetime.

INDEX